The Heart of the Ngoni

THE HEART OF THE NGONI

HEROES OF THE AFRICAN KINGDOM OF SEGU

BY
HAROLD COURLANDER
WITH
OUSMANE SAKO

UNIVERSITY OF MASSACHUSETTS PRESS AMHERST

First paperback edition, 1994
by the University of Massachusetts Press

Printed in the United States of America
ISBN 0–87023–929–5
LC 94–236

Library of Congress Cataloging-in-Publication Data

The Heart of the Ngoni: heroes of the African kingdom of Segu / by
    Harold Courlander with Ousmane Sako. —1st pbk. ed.
        p.   cm.
    Includes bibliographical references.
    Contents: The dawning of Segu — Ngolo Diara, who became a
king of Segu —Bassadjalan Zambele and the heroes of Kala —
Sokufo Seriba, a djeli of Segu — Da Djera and Da Monzon against
Samaniana Bassi — Da Monzon against Chiaro Mamari — Sekuruna
Toto's proposal to Da Monzon — The epic of Rakaridjan Kone, a
hero of Segu — In praise of Malamini Sinsani — Diuladjan Biabi, a
Soninke hero of Kiban — Tuba's last effort against Kiban.
        ISBN 0–87023–929–5 (pbk.: alk. paper)
        1. Bambara (African people)—Folklore. 2. Soninke (African
people)—Folklore. 3. Legends—Mali—Ségou (Region). 4. Ségou
(Mali: Region)—History. 5. Tales—Mali—Ségou (Region)
I. Courlander, Harold, 1908–   . II. Sako, Ousmane.
GR350.32.B3H47   1994
398.2'096623—dc20   94–236
                                                        CIP

CONTENTS

ACKNOWLEDGMENTS

The authors express their appreciation to the various djeli and other persons of knowledge who provided the narrations or information about the Bambara kingdom of Segu. In particular, thanks are given to Cheikna Amala Diabi, great grandson of Diuladjan Diabi; Sekou Souare of Kiban; Noumou Demba Toure; Deyi Baba Diallo; Djeli Baba Sissoko; and, for narrations given long ago, Djeli Ngolo Traore of Sinsani and Djeli Nti Diarra of Segu. We also voice sincere thanks to Harold Berman of Washington, D.C., and David McDowell of Nashville, Tennessee, for reading our book in manuscript and offering helpful editorial comments and suggestions.

"*Kings, blacksmiths and slaves can forget, but the heart of the ngoni remembers everything.*"

—FROM A SONG BY A SONINKE BARD

"*Great events do not occur every day,*
Therefore we sing of them for generations."

—FROM A SONG BY A BARD OF SEGU

THE
HEART
OF
THE
NGONI

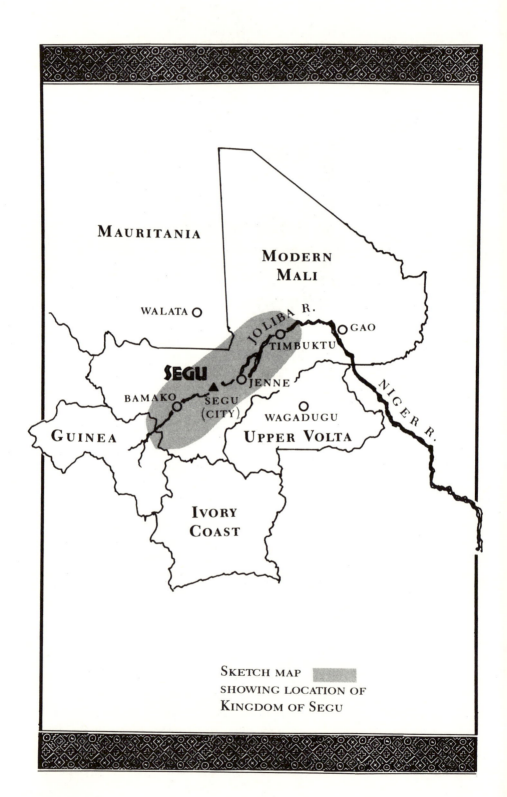

MAURITANIA

MODERN
MALI

WALATA ○

JOLIBA R.

SEGU

○ GAO

TIMBUKTU ○

BAMAKO ○
SEGU
(CITY)

○ JENNE

○ WAGADUGU

UPPER VOLTA

NIGER R.

GUINEA

IVORY
COAST

SKETCH MAP
SHOWING LOCATION OF
KINGDOM OF SEGU

INTRODUCTION

These heroic narratives are a journey into the life and oral literature of the Bambara, or Bamana, and Soninke peoples of Segu, a Sudanic kingdom that spanned nearly three centuries and finally disintegrated under pressure from Muslim and French colonial conquerors. Born on the banks of the Upper Niger, which the Bambara called Joliba, early in the seventeenth century, its precise beginnings shrouded in mystery and legend, Segu was created out of the same restless energy that in earlier centuries had produced the empires of Ghana, Mali and Songhay. Its founders were Bambara, but as the kingdom grew it absorbed numerous Soninke and Fula cities and lands.

For more than a thousand years the Western Sudan had been the scene of migrations, merging of peoples, political surgings and conflicts. City-states, kingdoms and empires arose, lived and withered away, their fragments reshaping themselves into new political centers powered by a continuing, unspent vitality. There surely were stretches of time when confrontation and war did not mar the land, but the oral history measures the passage of centuries by a succession of conflicts, wanderings and martial events. Heroes and their feats are the mnemonics by which great happenings are recalled, and, in the telling, it sometimes seems as though the heroes were not so much participants in events as they were creators of events. The songs sung by the djeli—the bard-historians—often are eulogies commemorating the accomplishments of men whose valor, chivalry and honor have left an imprint on heart and mind.

The people of Segu were related culturally and linguistically to other Mande groups that in earlier days figured prominently in the rise and fall of city-states, kingdoms and empires in this part of Africa. Ancient Ghana rose in this region in the fourth or fifth century A.D. under the control of the Soninke (sometimes called Maraka by the Bambara, and Sarakole by Europeans), and lasted possibly more than eight hundred years. It was succeeded by the Manding (Malinke) empire of Mali, which declined in the fifteenth century, and then by the empire of Songhay, which survived approximately to the beginning of the seventeenth century. Each of these empires at one time or another claimed authority and control over the peoples, villages, cities and lands between the Upper Niger and the River Senegal. It was in the same vicinity, on the west bend of the Niger, that Segu emerged early in the seventeenth century.

By this time the Malinke, the Soninke and the neighboring Fula, among other tribes, largely had become Islamized. The Bambara of Segu, as well as those of the more northerly Bambara kingdom called Kaarta, stubbornly resisted the tide of Islam. In Muslim usage the name Bambara was a synonym for fetishists or unbelievers. Although many of the wars undertaken by Muslim leaders were ostensibly efforts to impose the word of Mohammed on all parts of the Sudan, the old, familiar motivations were always present—attempts to gain control of important trade routes, to enhance political and economic control of a region, to extend the outer edges of a city-state or kingdom, or to destroy the military capabilities of potentially dangerous competitors. Implicit evidence in some of the epic narrations tells us, as well, that a king might launch a war because his professional fighters were becoming troublesome and restive under conditions of peace, or because he himself felt the need of enhancing his prestige.

2

In its two-and-a-half or three centuries of life Segu had many kings. Understandably, the oral history, transmitted primarily by the djeli, or bards, contains numerous contradictions, and it would be almost impossible to produce a reasonably accurate chronology of kings. There is widespread agreement that three brothers named Ngolo were the original settlers (but not kings) of Segu, though a variant account says that Biton Mamari Kulibali, who arrived several generations later, was the founder. The bardic and popular accounts nevertheless are in accord in naming the outstanding kings, including Biton Mamari Kulibali, Da Djera, Da Monzon and Ngolo Diara. Many great men whom the Bambara remember as heroes were not kings, however, but persons of noble birth who sought to prove their valor and honor in the context of the ongoing warfare between city-states and kingdoms.

The narrations in this book are recollections of deeds performed by some of these heroes. They are fragments of history and legend that do not necessarily dovetail neatly. Still, they tell us a great deal about Bambara values and institutions, about what was regarded as just or unjust, honorable or dishonorable, worthwhile or unmeritorious. They also reveal much about the Bambara concept of a universe in which the natural and the supernatural are aspects of a unitary life force. Again and again they stress the importance of destiny in the fortunes of heroes and, by implication, all other people. In the words of one bardic song:

> *If you are born to be great, you will be great.*
> *Therefore let us not concern ourselves with questions.*
> *If you are born not to be great, you will not be great.*
> *Therefore let us not concern ourselves with questions.*
> *If you are born to be ill, you will be ill.*
> *Therefore let us not concern ourselves with questions.*
> *If you are born to be strong, you will be strong.*
> *Therefore let us not concern ourselves with questions.*

Heroes in the Bambara tradition (as with other Sudanic peoples) generally came from the topmost social class known as ōron (called horo by the Malinke). In English translation the term is frequently given as "nobles." The word is not altogether satisfactory, but easier

3

to handle than, say, "citizens of the highest class," those above a group of "freeborn" castes who were masters of highly skilled crafts and arts.

As customarily described, the Bambara society was structured with the ōron or nobles at the top, followed by the grouping called nyamakala, which included hereditary professionals who normally married within their own caste group. The bard-historians, called djeli, had the highest rank among the nyamakala, followed by the blacksmiths, who also worked in gold and wood, then by the leatherworkers, then by other classes of artisans. The nyamakala as well as the ōron were regarded as freeborn. The lowest rung on the ladder consisted of slaves, who were considered noncitizens without rights or protections. Nobles generally married within the noble class so that their children would not be regarded as half nobles with diminished prestige. But it was possible for a noble male to marry a woman of, say, the djeli or blacksmith caste if he was willing to bear scoldings and abuse from his family. However, a noble male who married a slave woman was usually rejected by and in effect cut off from his family. A male slave normally married within the slave caste. On occasion he might marry a woman from one of the artisan castes, but never a daughter of a noble family. Paradoxically, many slaves, because they were captured in war, might have been able to trace their line of descent from important, freeborn families of the Sudan—Malinke, Soninke or Fula. Special social groupings existed outside this formal structure, such as the magic makers, or practitioners of the mystical sciences, and the Fula herdsmen who were entrusted with care of the cattle.

As a general proposition, a freeborn man might qualify himself as a hero by performing an outstanding deed that raised him above the level of ordinary persons. Thus, a rich man living thirty miles from the river had a canal constructed to bring water to his fields, and this accomplishment was so extraordinary that it motivated djeli to compose praise songs and play the ngoni (a plucked stringed instrument) in his honor. Usually, however, the hero was a man who accomplished exceptional deeds in war, or in personal combats against other heroes. The hero as an idealized figure not only had to be courageous in battle, but also had to have civic virtues. He was supposed to be generous, respectful and considerate. Modesty in heroes was admired, though exhibition of pride in difficult situations was expected, and when heroes came together in drinking fests, boasting was routine.

All nobles, and heroes foremost, were governed by a code of chivalry probably unsurpassed in the traditions of other peoples. When heroes came together in individual combat, a number of courtesies were observed. It was a matter not only of skill against skill and valor against valor, but of magic against magic. Each of the fighters possessed both offensive and defensive magical attributes. As seen in some of the narratives in this collection, it was commonplace for one hero to offer the other the opportunity to strike first, possibly giving him three shots from his gun. This was a test of magical protections. Afterward, the second hero would take his turn. If bullets failed to be effective, the fighters would then resort to knives, cutlasses or other weapons. Once battle had been joined, there was no turning back, and the winner was expected to take the loser's head.

It was considered dishonorable for a noble to fight someone whom he knew to be afraid of him. If he discovered his opponent's fear before challenging him, he would not make the challenge. If he made the discovery at the moment of combat he would turn and ride away. In a gesture of chivalric generosity a hero might reveal to another what his magical protections were and how he might be killed. Sometimes a young hero declined to fight an older man who resembled his father. In some of the narratives chivalric generosity goes beyond what anyone has a right to expect, as in "Bassadjalan Zambele and the Heroes of Kala." A hunter who challenges Bassadjalan is unsuccessful in killing him because of Bassadjalan's magical protections, and he excuses himself on the grounds that he forgot to make a sacrifice to his talisman. Bassadjalan asks what is needed for the sacrifice. The hunter says that kola nuts are needed, but that he does not have any. Thereupon Bassadjalan gives him the required kolas, the hunter makes the sacrificial offering and tries again.

The chivalric code was observed not only in individual combat, but also in wars between armies. An attacking army might make an appointment with its adversary, announcing a "visit" on a certain day. Arriving at the walls of the adversary's city, the attackers would extend courteous greetings and receive greetings in return. As in "Da Monzon Against Chiaro Mamari," if the defending city was not ready to begin fighting, the attackers waited patiently in their camp. Battles usually began at daybreak and continued until nightfall. If an attacking army arrived at a city's walls in late afternoon, it was too late to begin and the fighting was deferred until the next morning. Meanwhile the attackers were invited inside the city for an evening of feasting and drinking, and before daybreak they would return to their camp, take up their weapons and prepare for battle.

A hero story without reference to the djeli (called by the term griots in much of the existing literature) is nearly unthinkable. These singers and keepers of history had hereditary ties to noble families. A djeli transmitted to one of his sons all the knowledge he had about the noble family he served, taught him how to play the ngoni and other instruments, and rehearsed him in the art of singing the wolosekoro, a form reserved for praise songs to or about heroes. On the death of the djeli, the son would be prepared to take his place. If the djeli was thus irrevocably tied by birth to serving a noble family, the family also had ties and responsibilities to the djeli that could not be severed. He was the repository of the family's history, its accomplishments and its lineage—in short, the proof of its authentic nobility.

In addition to being the family chronicler, its musician and its praiser, the djeli was relied upon for many important services. If there was a dispute within the family, the djeli might be called on to mediate. And if the family wanted a certain young woman as a wife for one of its sons, the djeli might be sent to make the request and the arrangements. He was rewarded generously for his services, usually with gifts of cowries, livestock, land or slaves. A djeli was not backward about making requests to the family he served. If he needed a horse or money he asked for it. For a rich man the gifts were no problem, and giving generously to a djeli enhanced one's prestige, as is dramatized in the story, "In Praise of Malamini Sinsani."

But for others not so well off, a djeli's demands could be burdensome. In current popular belief, if a djeli were asked what he would like to have as a reward for an excellent rendering of a family's chronology and exploits, he might ask for an extravagant gift such as forty cows, or twenty slaves, or the master's charmed weapons, and in honor, and perhaps out of anxiety, it would have to be given. There was an ever-present risk in failing to satisfy a djeli's expectations. A disgruntled djeli might insert into his praise songs some event or episode that derogated the family lineage. He might say, for example, that a certain ancestor was not "the son of his father," meaning that he was a bastard, and this would imply that the family did not have true noble blood.

A djeli in the service of a king had special prestige and influence. In addition to being the official historian and chronicler of the king's family (and therefore of the kingdom), he served as the "transmitter of words." Anyone addressing the king in a formal assemblage made his statement to, and received the king's response through, the djeli. The djeli, though not a noble, was sometimes one of the king's counselors, and on occasion acted as a royal emissary or ambassador.

The importance of the blacksmith, or numuke, in traditional Bambara society is only vaguely hinted at in these narrations. First, of course, he provided the tools of work and the weapons of war, as well as objects made of gold and silver. Even wood was part of his domain; he carved doors, utensils, spear shafts, fetish figures and ceremonial masks. He explored for earth containing iron ore and smelted it. During the period alluded to in the hero stories he made guns and gunpowder. In short, he was the central figure of Bambara technology.

Yet technology was the physical expression of an invisible spiritual force. The blacksmith and his caste were believed to possess this force. Not only did it give him the power to work metals, it was transmitted through him to the knives, swords and guns that he forged. Thus we hear of the mystic powers given to weapons by the blacksmith, as well as the flow of force into fetish figures and masks. Women of the blacksmith caste were believed to possess particularly potent mystical strength related to the processing of iron. We are told of male smelters who opened their smelting furnaces only to find that the ore had produced no iron whatsoever. The cause of the failure was believed to be the absence of adequate spiritual force. To remedy things, the blacksmith would go to his sister or some other woman of the caste and ask for help. She, in turn, would perform a ceremony, after which the blacksmith would return to his furnace

7

and find that iron had appeared in the fire. In addition to other ceremonial duties, the blacksmith was in charge of circumcisions at manhood initiations.

The role of magic in the fortunes of heroes already has been noted. Young men were cautioned again and again that it was not enough to possess martial skills and valor, but that they needed the help of the "mystic sciences" to offset the magic of their enemies. Contests between heroes or between armies were ultimately decided by four elements: skill or intelligence, courage, destiny and magic. The narratives do not seem to suggest that chance or accident played a significant part in the outcome of martial conflicts.

The magic makers—practitioners of the "mystic sciences"—primarily were Muslim morikes (sometimes called almamis), teachers and interpreters of the Koran, and their non-Muslim Bambara counterparts, the filelikelas. These persons were also diviners. Koranic knowledge was considered especially important in giving weapons extraordinary powers and in providing human bodies with supernatural protection. Every town and city had its morikes and filelikelas, but sometimes a person traveled a great distance to consult a famous practitioner, perhaps as far as Timbuktu or beyond.

The narratives give us only fleeting pictures of slave life, but it seems clear that slavery was an integral and important part of the Bambara society. Slaves could be bought or taken in war. A noble captured in combat could be reduced to a slave status that was passed on to his descendants. He was considered property and had no clearly defined rights. He could be kept, sold or given away, and the severity of his life depended on the character of the master. Some slaves were treated well, some badly. Anyone apprehending a runaway slave could claim him as his own, much as cattle could be seized if they invaded a noble's fields. Field slaves are said to have lived in their own community in a designated quarter of the town. They had no expectation or hope of bettering their position. Perhaps the best fortune that could come to a male or female slave was to be made a personal attendant to a chief, a wealthy man, a hero, a king or his favorite wife.

That Segu was a kingdom with flourishing trade (though with the familiar contrasts between rich and poor) is testified to in the journals of Mungo Park, who traveled through Bambara country in 1795 (and again ten years later) during the reign of Da Monzon (rendered as Mansong).* Describing Segu City, the journals tell us:

> Sego, the capital of Bambarra, at which I had now arrived, consists, properly speaking, of four distinct towns; two on the northern bank of the Niger, called Sego Korro and Sego Boo; and two on the southern bank, called Sego Soo Korro and Sego See Korro. They are all surrounded with high mud walls; the houses are built of clay, of a square form, with flat roofs; some of them have two storeys, and many of them are whitewashed. Besides these buildings, Moorish mosques are seen in every quarter; and the streets, though narrow, are broad enough for every useful purpose, in a country where wheel-carriages are entirely unknown. From the best inquiries I could make, I have reason to believe that Sego contains altogether about thirty thousand inhabitants. The king of Bambarra constantly resides at Sego See Korro; he employs a great many slaves in conveying people over the river, and the money they receive (though the fare is only ten cowrie shells for each individual) furnishes a considerable revenue to the king in the course of a year. The canoes are of a singular construction, each of them being formed of the trunks of two large trees, rendered concave, and joined together, not side by side, but end ways; the junction being exactly across the middle of the canoe; they are therefore very long and disproportionably narrow, and have neither decks nor masts; they are, however, very roomy; for I observed in one of them four horses, and several people crossing over the river. When we arrived at this ferry, with a view to pass over to that part of the town in which the king resides, we found a great number waiting for a passage; they looked at me with silent wonder, and I distinguished, with concern, many Moors among them. There were three different places of embarkation, and the ferrymen were very diligent and expeditious;

*Travels in Africa, edited by Ronald Miller, London, J. M. Dent and Sons, 1954, 1969, pp. 149–50.

but, from the crowd of people, I could not immediately obtain a passage; and sat down upon the bank of the river, to wait for a more favourable opportunity. The view of this extensive city; the numerous canoes upon the river; the crowded population, and the cultivated state of the surrounding country, formed altogether a prospect of civilisation and magnificence, which I little expected to find in the bosom of Africa.

Mungo Park probably saw Segu at its most flourishing moment. Early in the nineteenth century Muslim "reformers" swept through this region of the Sudan, ostensibly to bring Bambara pagans, among others, under the rule of Islam. Led by a Fula warrior chief named al-Hajj Omar, Muslim armies composed of believers of various tribes subdued the cities of Segu and the capital itself. The kingdom of Segu survived in name, but its government passed from the hands of Bambara ruling families, and it became merely a part of a shifting, changing political landscape. Segu had emerged out of the fragments of earlier (and greater) kingdoms and began to merge again with the restless surflike surgings that had characterized the Sudan for more than a millennium.

Al-Hajj Omar ruled, and after him his nephew, Ahmadu ibn Tindani (also known as Ahmadu Seku). But the possibility of a new kingdom shaping itself out of the old no longer existed, because by this time France had undertaken the conquest and colonization of this portion of the African continent. The story of Diuladjan Diabi brings us well into the period of the Muslim rule of Segu, before the French had yet taken control. The final brief story, "Tuba's Last Effort Against Kiban," set in the period of French colonial rule, is a nostalgic reminder of the earlier days of Segu heroes.

THE DAWNING OF SEGU

EFORE A CHILD IS BORN he does not yet
exist. Before a city-state is born it does not yet
exist. Who knows the nature of a child yet to be
born a hundred years from now? Who knows his
name, or whether he will be a hero or a slave? The
secret of his identity and his character will be
hidden from us until he appears among the people of the earth. A
city-state does not appear through all the centuries. The mind of
man cannot conceive it because it is not perceived with the eyes. And
then one day it rises in the bush, standing on a hill or at the edge of a
river. It thrives, it becomes great; or perhaps it dies away and its
walls crumble and are covered again with the grass of the bush. Yet
great cities and great heroes do not truly die, for they remain alive in
the songs of the bards. It is said: "Momentous things do not happen
every day. Therefore we sing of them father to son and generation to
generation."

11

But those cities and people of the future, how can they be known to the mind of man? Only for the architect of the universe do they exist, and they will be seen by human eyes only after all the threads are drawn together to make them visible. The winds blow, the clouds drift, the rains fall, trails through the forest are made and abandoned, mankind lives on. The hunter hunts and the farmer tills his fields. Blacksmiths make hoes for peace and spears for war. Heroes go from place to place in the hope of proving their courage and honor. All is the same, nothing changes.

And at a certain moment, seemingly out of nothing, a house appears, then a village, then a city, perhaps a kingdom or an empire. Who can say that it was not there all the time? Who can say that the architect did not touch a finger to the void of time and say, "Here is a city to come"? Let us remember that a city is not merely a wall surrounding a noisy marketplace. It is made of families, and every family is a story in itself; of people hunting game, and every hunt is a story in itself; of grain stored in granaries, every grain brought there from a field, carried by a woman or a girl; of hoes, every hoe forged in a fire by a blacksmith; of fishermen, who have learned the secrets of the river from their fathers; and of heroes defending the walls, some living on, some passing into night. All things are tied, and they have been brought together in a fragment of time to make the city or the kingdom visible.

In such a way it happened that a small village appeared at the edge of the Joliba River, known to some as the Niger, and out of that village there grew a city and an empire known as Segu. It was founded by hunters from Manding, yet others had opened the trail before them. Mystical events determined where Segu would rise and how long it would live. In time, the kingdom spread to the north, south, east and west. And the djeli, or bards, say in their songs that it extended from Segu Kora to Sansibara; from Segu Kora to Woroguda; from Segu Kora to the country of Sahel; and from Sefala to Kurusabana.

Now, the djeli who recited events in the life of Segu were many. Some were djeli of the villages, some were djeli of the king's court, some were Mandinka, some were Soninke and some were Bambara. Some told the story of Segu one way, some told it another. So there is no single account of the dawning of Segu on which all djeli agree. Still, all tell of the Ngolo brothers, and no one contests that Biton Mamari Kulibali was the first true king of Segu.

The story begins when the city of Wagadu, in the country of the Soninke, was living in all its splendor. Its fields produced rich harvests, and traders came to that city from all directions to deal in cloth, gold and wares from distant lands. In Wagadu were great markets, and portions of the city were set aside for blacksmiths, goldsmiths, leatherworkers and craftsmen of all kinds. Many languages were heard in the streets—Manding, Fula, Hausa, Arabic and others. There were scholars, Muslim teachers of the Koran, and practitioners of the mystic sciences. The name Wagadu signified "infinitely deep," and it was in fact such a city, complex and profound in its variety and wonders. Whatever men sought after, they went to Wagadu to find.

Living in the city was Segu Almami, a Fula teacher of the Koran. Because his knowledge of mystic sciences was great, he was also a morike. The mystic sciences were of importance in the lives of the people, and they went to a morike whenever they needed protection against an enemy, feared for their crops or wanted to know something about the future. The morike would employ his knowledge and sometimes ask Allah for assistance. Segu Almami was popular in Wagadu, and he had many students. Each day they came and sat to hear him explain the meanings of the Koran and other Muslim writings. One day he announced to his students that he was taking them on a journey. He said, "Wagadu is great, yet the world in which it sits is greater still. Wagadu is infinitely deep, yet the world that surrounds it is infinitely wide. We will make a journey and see the wonders of the universe. In this way we shall heighten our understanding of the Koran."

So Segu Almami led his students on a pilgrimage of learning, traveling along the watercourse of the River Joliba. Whenever they saw a certain animal of the bush, or a certain plant, or an outcropping of rock, or a termite hill, Segu Almami would speak of it and explain its part in the plan of life. One day when they stopped for their afternoon prayer, the morike saw a large stone glistening in the sunlight. He said to his students, "Here we see something not to be found in Wagadu. The large glittering stone is solid gold. How it comes to be resting here I cannot tell you. But I see something behind it that is not visible to others. A devil stands there to guard it. He holds a spear in his hand." One of the students said, "Almami, I see no one standing there. I see only the stone." And the Almami answered, "Yes, it is not visible to you. Thus we learn something at this place. The world is made up of two things: what the senses perceive and what they are incapable of perceiving. It is knowledge and faith in Allah that make us aware of objects and beings that cast no shadows. What is told to me is that here there is a great unexplained force, and that here, some day, a powerful kingdom will rise out of the bush."

The morike and his students continued their pilgrimage. But before they had traveled far, one of the young men decided to go back for a piece of the gold stone. He gave his headload to a friend, saying, "Hold this for a moment. I must go into the bush and relieve myself." He went into the bush, but instead of returning immediately he went back to the stone of gold and tried to break off a small piece for himself. He did not see what the morike had seen, the invisible devil standing there with his invisible spear. The devil killed the young man, and his invisible spear left an invisible wound. When Segu Almami discovered that his student was missing, he saw in his mind a picture of the young man's body lying by the golden stone. So he returned to the place, and it was just as he had known it would be.

The morike and his students buried the body, and when that was done they placed the golden stone as a headmarker for the grave. The morike took a pen and container of ink from his knapsack, and he inscribed a message on the stone which read: "I, Almami Segu, leave this writing to be read by others in some future time. This spot has a divine and mystic force. If a city is established here it will prosper and become great. It will live for many generations, and will be remembered by the djeli in their songs forever. Because it is I who give you this information, let the city take my name, Segu."

After that, the morike led his students back to Wagadu. Thus was spun one of the threads out of which the kingdom of Segu was woven, but it was only a single thread, and other threads yet remained to be spun.

Centuries passed, and it happened that four hunters of the town of Walata in Sahel, now called Mauritania, went on a journey to the south. The eldest of the four was named Bedari, and he was their chief. They became lost, and after many months they came to a large river, the Joliba, though they did not know its name. By chance they discovered the rock of gold, and they read the inscription written thereon by the morike of Wagadu, Segu Almami. Bedari said to his hunters, "This is a wonderful thing that is written here. We are a long way from Walata. Why should we return there? Let us remain here and make a settlement. We will see if the prophecy is fulfilled. Perhaps we will prosper." They discussed it. They argued. But a time came when they were in agreement. So at that place each of them built a small hut for himself. They lived there, and made the place their hunting camp. They hunted, they lived on.

One day they saw a large party of men approaching along the riverbank. They greeted the travelers and gave them dried meat to eat. Bedari asked them, "Where do you come from and where are you going?" One of the travelers answered, "We come from anywhere and go anywhere. We have no village." Bedari asked, "What man does not have a village?" They replied, "All villages are ours." Hearing that, Bedari understood that these men led an outlaw life, raiding one village or another for food and plunder. He said, "Aaaah! It is a hard way of living." They answered, "Yes, it is hard. But we have been living this way for many years. We can never go home. Where we came from, they do not want us anymore. So this is our life."

Bedari looked at them one by one. He saw they were young. He spoke to them as a father, saying, "Aaaah, you young men, what is there to look forward to in your lives? You have no homes or wives of your own. You will have no families in your old age. We four hunters have not been here very long, but we will soon clear fields and grow crops." The travelers said, "What? Here in the bush? We do not see any village, only four poor huts." Bedari answered, "Before a village is built, there is no village. Before the bush is cleared there are no farms. A morike of Wagadu has prophesied that a powerful force will produce a great city here where we stand. That is why we hunters are staying."

The travelers slept, and in the morning they said to Bedari, "We

15

heard what you said. We are tired of the life we have been living. We reflected on your invitation. We will stay." Bedari said, "You are welcome, on one condition. You must pledge to put your former lives behind you and conduct yourselves as good citizens." They answered, "Yes, we agree to what you say."

So the men built houses for themselves and began to clear land for their fields. Yet though they built a village, it was not quite a village, because there were no women there. But the threads of Segu were drawing together. One day a party of women appeared on the bank of the river, going hurriedly from one place to another. When they saw the men of Segu they cried out in alarm, "Aaaah! Now we are finished!" Bedari calmed them, saying, "Why are you running like this? Who is pursuing you?" The eldest woman spoke for them. She said, "Our village was attacked by a pillaging army. Our men were all killed or taken as slaves. We women escaped into the bush. We were helpless without anyone to protect us, and we ran in fear of what might happen. Now it seems that we are in your hands. We cannot run any further."

Bedari replied, "Do not fear the worst. There is no danger here. We are decent people." The hunters fed the women and calmed them. Afterward Bedari said, "It happens that in our village, which we call Segu, there are no women. We need wives to make everything complete. We will not treat you as slaves. If you accept a man he will be your husband. We will have families and Segu will grow." The women discussed it among themselves. They had confidence in Bedari's words. At last they said, "Yes, we will stay." And when it came to the choosing, it turned out that there were fifty-four women and fifty-four men, so every man had a wife and every woman had a husband. Bedari himself chose the woman who had spoken for the others, and he conducted the proper ceremony so that the marriages were true.

Bedari was recognized by all as the chief of the village. Children were born. The village increased, and the grain grew plentifully in the fields. Bedari had a son named Trokomari. And when Bedari's time on earth was consumed, when the light of day faded for him, Trokomari was sixteen years old. Though he was too young to rule a village, still the people accepted Trokomari as chief because of the respect they owed his father. Trokomari had no depth of under-

standing. He played with the chieftainship as if he were playing with
a toy, and out of his hearing people sometimes called him the "child-
king."

The songs of the djeli in later days did not speak well of
Trokomari. They tell that Trokomari issued an order that whoever
might trespass on his peanut field would be sentenced to death. If a
man walked by mistake into Trokomari's peanut field, he was
executed. If a cow wandered into Trokomari's peanut field and
nibbled at the leaves of the plants, Trokomari had it killed. If a
chicken pecked at the ground in Trokomari's peanut field, Trokomari had it killed. In time it came to be that if someone died of an
unknown cause, people would say, "Aaaah! Perhaps he has been
eating Trokomari's peanuts."

This was what occurred after Bedari died. Sometimes it happens
that a child exceeds his father; sometimes it happens that a child
does not have the good character of his father, as in the case of
Trokomari. Yet Trokomari was a link between the beginning and the
end, and in time the kingdom of Segu would appear, in all its glory,
out of the wasteland of the bush.

Living in the country of the Manding in the town of Djarokoroba
was a man called Mbari Kulibali. Mbari Kulibali had three wives, all
from the village of Dja. One was named Nya, another Barama and
the third Tolun. Each of the wives had a son, and all of the sons
were given the same name, Ngolo. To distinguish one Ngolo from
another, each of them prefixed his name with that of his mother.
And so there were Nya Ngolo, Barama Ngolo and Tolun Ngolo.
They also added their father's name, Kulibali. Now, it is commonplace that brothers by the same father and different mothers do
not get along well with one another, but with the three Ngolos it was
different. They grew together in friendship, together learned the
arts of living, together learned the use of weapons, and were
inseparable companions.

In their childhood and youth they listened to the djeli, the bards
who played the ngoni and sang wolosekoro, those songs about

the courageous accomplishments of heroes of earlier days. The wolosekoro told not only of combats and the thrust of spears. They stressed the importance of good character, the virtues of harmony and generosity, and the existence of mystic forces in the universe. They taught that while young men must strive, they needed the knowledge that only the old could give them. They taught that each person had his own destiny, whether to be a blacksmith, a diviner, a farmer, a hero or a king, and they said that if a man lived his life honorably he need never fear evil words spoken about him. These were the teachings by which the Ngolo brothers grew to manhood.

The songs of the djeli do not agree as to why the brothers departed from Djarokoroba, but it is said that they went on a long journey to the east, where they learned something of war and achieved honor for themselves. After a long absence, they decided to return to Manding, even perhaps to Djarokoroba where they were born. Because they had distinguished themselves in war, the Ngolo brothers now had a following of soldiers and hunters, and so they made their way across the land in a large party. They passed through the city of Gao on the River Joliba, and they journeyed on to Timbuktu. From Timbuktu they followed the river southward, but before reaching Manding they arrived in the country of Segu, which was then ruled by the "child-king," Trokomari.

Their journey had been long, and the Ngolo brothers and their followers decided to stay in this country a while to rest. So Barama Ngolo, Nya Ngolo and Tolun Ngolo went to see Trokomari. They said, "We are traveling a long journey. We come from Manding, and we are on our way back to our town, Djarokoroba. We ask your permission to remain here a while. Give us a place for our village and land for our fields. We have many strong fighters among us, and we will help to defend Segu if it is attacked."

Trokomari gave his permission, and he designated an area of the bush where they could settle. So the brothers took their followers to that place, built houses and cleared fields. They called their village Anserakola, meaning "We have accomplished something," but later the name became shortened to Sekola. While they were clearing the bush they discovered four fetish shrines. One belonged to the jinns of the bush; another belonged to the river jinns; another belonged to the "little jinns," who were only three feet in height; and the fourth was a fetish to which farmers could appeal for bountiful crops. Near the fetishes they found three spears to which were affixed medicine bags and other mystical objects, which the three brothers understood to be symbols of martial endowment.

After discussing the matter, the Ngolo brothers went to the chief of Segu and reported what they had discovered. They said, "The land we are clearing is your land. Everything in Segu is yours. Therefore we want to tell you about the fetishes and mystic spears. What shall we do with them?" Trokomari did not comprehend the meaning of what they had found. He said, "What have such things to do with me?" The brothers argued with Trokomari. They said the objects were of great value, but Trokomari was stubborn. He said, "I do not want them." The Ngolo brothers knew that a chief could not renounce fetishes in such an offhand manner. So they proposed a gambling game with Trokomari, with the winner taking the fetishes. Trokomari agreed. Using a kola nut for a gambling piece, they played. The brothers won and Trokomari lost. Therefore the brothers became the proper owners of the fetishes and spears.

The village of Sekola took form and grew. People living in isolation in the bush came and settled in the village. Some people moved to Sekola from Segu itself. The population increased until more land was needed for farms. So the Ngolo brothers went again to request more land from Trokomari. He assigned more land to them, and they built a new village and called it Sekurayara, meaning "Our power increases." In time the name became shortened to Sekoro. Still once again the brothers asked for land for a new village, and this one they named Seguguna, meaning "Our power becomes great." So now there were three villages that had been founded by the Ngolos, and they all thrived.

In the original village of Segu, however, the young chief, Trokomari, ruled by whim rather than by reason. He did not accept the advice of the old men. Because he had the power to do so, he abused people's rights. His justice was unpredictable, and no one knew what he was going to do next. Trokomari's djeli tried to guide him. He sang, "Play with the world, and the world will play with you," meaning that if Trokomari did not take his responsibilities seriously, people would not take him seriously. The djeli sang, "The world is a stern mother with its child," meaning that the community would not forever tolerate Trokomari's poor behavior. But Trokomari heard nothing. People advised him to marry so that he would have a son to succeed him. He did not hear. He learned nothing. He went on as though he would live forever, not perceiving that a twig can be broken in the middle just as it can be broken at the end. When death crept upon Trokomari it surprised him, because he was not ready. When he died, Segu had no chief to lead it. So the people sent a message to the Ngolo brothers asking them to take responsibility for Segu. The Ngolo brothers accepted. The eldest of the three, Barama Ngolo, became the chief, and he ruled the four villages—Sekoro, Sekola, Seguguna and Segu—not as a king would, but as the leader of a confederation.

Thus the kola nuts thrown anciently upon a divining tray by a long-forgotten filelikela were becoming visible to human eyes. Each kola fell and lay in a particular place, and the filelikela saw the prophecy in each of them. One kola was the Almami Segu living in Wagadu. Another was the golden stone on which he inscribed his words. Four were the hunters from Walata. Three others were the Ngolo brothers from Djarokoroba. There, on the divining tray of the ancient filelikela, was everything that was to happen, every wanderer to reach Segu, every footprint on every trail. Only now could the meaning be faintly seen by men. Out of the sea of time a kingdom was emerging. But it was not yet a kingdom, only the shadow of a kingdom, and its leader was Barama Ngolo Kulibali.

And now Barama Ngolo himself consulted a filelikela about the four fetishes and the three spears that had been found in the bush when the brothers first arrived. The filelikela took sixty-four kolas from his leather bag and spilled them on the ground and read their meaning. He said, "The three spears represent the power of the three brothers of the Kulibali family who planted the seed of the kingdom of Segu. They tell us that you and your brothers will succeed, and that each of you in turn will govern Segu. As for the four fetishes, they are the wild spirits of the bush, the spirits of the river, the little people of the forest, and the spirits of farming. They have great power for good or for evil. They must be placated.

Therefore, before Segu can thrive, a sacrifice must be made." And so in the seventh month after the rains came to an end there was a ceremony at the site of the fetishes and four animals were sacrificed. The fetishes were asked to bring children, good crops, health and long life to the people of Segu.

After some years had passed, Barama's brother Nya Ngolo said to him, "Older brother, I want to go out into the bush and establish a new farming center to extend the influence of Segu." Barama Ngolo consented, and he gave his brother two hundred thirty settlers and also a party of hunters for security. Nya Ngolo took his people into the bush and founded a village called Djawkoni. Then Tolun Ngolo likewise asked permission to establish a new farming center. Barama Ngolo agreed, and he gave his brother a similar number of settlers and hunters, and Tolun's village took the name Geya.

So Segu's influence gradually expanded through the countryside, but no man outlives time, and Barama Ngolo grew old and a day came when the light faded for him. When Barama died his brother Nya Ngolo succeeded him as chief, and when Nya Ngolo died the chieftainship was taken over by Tolun Ngolo. Tolun also died in his time, and then the chieftainship of Segu went to Barama Ngolo's son, Dunu Mamari.

But Dunu Mamari had no child to be his heir. For thirty years his wife Sunu shared his bed with him but never became pregnant. Dunu Mamari consulted with the foremost filelikela in Segu. The filelikela performed mystic rituals, but nothing he did produced a child. One day Sunu went to her husband and asked permission to make a three-day journey, though without saying where she planned to go. Dunu Mamari agreed. Sunu then traveled to the Muslim town of Dja, where she arrived after dark. Now, the people of Segu were Bambara, and the Bambara were not Muslims. Yet Sunu went to the mosque in Dja, entered, placed her mat on the floor and slept. When the almami came before dawn to conduct the morning prayers, he found Sunu sleeping there. He woke her, saying, "Woman, what are you doing here?" Sunu, though she was not a Muslim, replied to the almami, "I have a credit with Allah, and I have come to ask Allah to make the credit good." The almami said, "You are saying that Allah owes you something?" Sunu replied, "Yes, that is why I am here."

21

The almami said, "Woman, are you not Bambara? Since when do pagans come to the mosque to make claims upon Allah?" Sunu answered, "Nevertheless, I have a claim to make." The almami said, "Very well, I hear you," meaning that he understood her words though he had still to hear the evidence. He said, "Woman, move to one side now so the people can pray. We will speak again later."

The mosque became crowded, and the prayers were said. Afterward, when the men were leaving, the almami said, "People of Dja, do not leave just yet. There is a woman here who claims that Allah owes her a debt. Stay and be witnesses to whatever she may tell us." Then he addressed Sunu, saying, "Woman, what is your name and where do you come from?" She answered, "I am Sunu and I come from Segu." He said to her, "Very well, explain to us why you believe Allah owes you something." Sunu replied, "In my village there are Muslim teachers who have come from among the Soninke and the Fula. They tell us that if a person lives a good life, Allah will reward him. I have lived in the way Allah says we should live. I have earned credit with Allah, and now I need something in return." The almami said, "Yes, we listen."

Sunu said: "When I was young, there were twenty-four marriageable girls in my village, but only ten were virgins and I was one of them. My husband was the first man I ever slept with, and since I married him I never slept with another man. If my husband ever spoke to me in confidence, I kept that confidence. If he ever asked my opinion, I gave it; if he did not ask my opinion I remained silent. Whatever I overheard him say to others, I put it away in my strongbox and left it there. If he admonished me to improve in some way, I improved. When he bathed, I did not merely bring a calabash of warm water and leave it sitting on the floor; I held the calabash for him until he was finished. Then I took the water away and disposed of it properly. When I prepared his meals, I came to him, kneeled and said, 'My husband, the food is ready.' If he was ready to eat, I brought the calabash of food and held it for him. When he was finished, only then did I eat. In all the years we were together, my husband never saw me sleeping. I did not close my eyes until he slept, and I arose before he awakened.

"It is said by the almamis in Segu that this is what Allah wants. But I never received my reward. I have been childless for thirty years. Other women in Segu, some not as virtuous as I have been, have two, three, perhaps five children. Yet I have none. Now you understand why I am here. I believe that Allah owes me a child." When the witnesses in the mosque heard Sunu's story, they agreed that she had lived according to Allah's wishes, and they asked the almami to do something for her. He said to Sunu, "Go home now, Sunu. Allah has his reasons. Whether he will give you a child or not, I cannot say. But I will take your part. I will ask Allah to consider everything you have told us."

Sunu then returned to Segu, and only then did she tell the chief what the purpose of her journey had been. Time passed. Sunu conceived a child. She said to her husband, "What the almami said was true. Allah has rewarded me for the credit I earned." The child who was born was a boy. When Sunu's family received the news, they were happy and astonished. They said, "Something exceptional has happened! After thirty years Sunu bears a child. Because of this he should be called Biton." In Bambara the word *biton* signifies "today again," meaning "after so much time has passed." In this way the boy acquired the name Biton Mamari Kulibali.

When his time came, the light faded for Dunu Mamari, and Biton Mamari became the ruler of all Segu. Because so many cities had sought the protection of Segu, it was extensive and powerful. The cities recognized Segu as a kingdom and Biton Mamari as its true king. Commerce flourished, and the River Joliba became a great highway for traders coming from Gao and Timbuktu in the north and Bamako in the south. The population of the capital city grew and spread out on both sides of the river. Segu had many artisans, scholars and doctors of the mystical sciences. Biton Mamari created a powerful army, called Tonjon, by recruiting nobles from all the cities of the kingdom. The name signified "association of slaves," but the soldiers were freemen and they were considered to be, rather than slaves, the protectors of Segu. Biton Mamari also introduced cowries as money, and families were taxed in cowries instead of in honey as in the time of his father. The djeli say that there were no great wars in Biton Mamari's day, for Segu was powerful and no city sought to challenge its authority.

Ngolo Diara, Who Became a King of Segu

N THE TIME OF BITON MAMARI, a chief by the
name of Yiriba ruled in the village of Niolla.
Living with him in his house was his younger
brother, Diara Dja, who was afflicted with an
illness that would not leave him. The chief,
Yiriba, looked for a wife for Diara Dja. But he was
not successful, because even though Diara Dja came from a noble
line, no family wanted to give its daughter to an ill man.

Diara Dja became discouraged and gave up hope of having a wife.
He spent his hours sitting or sleeping in the anteroom of the chief's
house. He would not go out and meet with other young men his age.
He did not have the spirit of living. If Yiriba said to him, "I hear that
such-and-such a family in such-and-such a village has a daughter. I
will send to find out about her," Diara Dja answered, "No, it is
useless. I am resigned not to marry. I will stay here. Let us leave
things as they are."

Time went by. Then one day some traders came to Niolla, and after they had sold their kola nuts and bought their salt, they visited the chief's house. There they met Diara Dja and spoke with him. When they heard why he had no wife or household of his own, they said, "You are wrong to sit here without hope. It is true that most noble families would be reluctant to give their daughter to a man with an illness. But that is not the end of the matter. Perhaps there is a young woman somewhere who is not married because she has an infirmity of her own, but who is strong and has a good character. She could be a good wife and give you children." Diara listened, thinking, "Perhaps what they say is true."

The traders spoke to the chief, telling him what they had told his younger brother. Yiriba also took hope, saying, "Yes, that is good. I thank you for saying it." The traders said, "Living in a village not far from here there is a young girl of a good family. She is healthy in every way except that she has a crippled foot. If you wish, we will go there and ask about her." Yiriba replied, "Yes, I wish it. I accept your offer." He gave money to the traders, and they went to the girl's village and spoke to her parents on behalf of Diara Dja. The parents agreed, and the girl consented to become Diara Dja's wife. After giving the parents presents, the traders brought the girl back to Niolla and presented her at the chief's house. Diara Dja and the girl were married. In time they had a son and a daughter. The boy's name was Ngolo, and he also took his father's name, so that he was called Ngolo Diara.

It happened one time, when Ngolo was four years old, that a filelikela of Niolla was divining with kola nuts for a certain person of the village, and the kolas revealed something that should not have appeared in that particular divination. The filelikela spoke of it to other practitioners of the mystical sciences. They agreed with him that the kolas prophesied that Ngolo Diara would some day become a king of Segu. When word of the prophecy came to the ears of Yiriba he became troubled. He thought, "I have four healthy sons, yet it is the single son of my sick younger brother who is prophesied to become a king. Everything that Diara Dja has, I have given him. It is not fair for Ngolo to become a king while my sons have no future like this awaiting them." And in the secret parts of his mind, Yiriba began to consider ways to be rid of Ngolo.

A time of the year came when the chief had to remit village taxes to the king in Segu. Though the taxes were in the form of cowries, they were called "the-price-of-the-honey," because they were in lieu of the honey that people formerly paid to the king. Yiriba sent his collector to gather the taxes from every family in Niolla. Diara Dja did not offer any cowries, because he owned little and was too ill to grow crops in the fields. Yiriba prepared for the journey to Segu City. He went to Diara Dja and said, "Well, now, my brother, I am taking the taxes to Biton Mamari. So give me the cowries you owe and I will take them along."

This was not proper, because when a person was ill and unable to work, the king excused him from paying the-price-of-the-honey. Diara Dja replied, "Older brother, how can I pay my tax? I am not able to work in the fields. I do not own anything. Perhaps you are joking." Yiriba said, "No, I am serious. The king has said, 'Let everyone pay his tax.' So I cannot excuse anyone." Diara Dja replied, "Older brother, I have no cowries to give." Yiriba said firmly, "I insist that you give something. Otherwise the king will hold it against me." Diara Dja said, "I own nothing worth anything. If you see something of value, take it."

Yiriba said, "Very well. I take you at your word. Give me your son Ngolo and I will give him to the king as your contribution." Diara Dja answered, "Ngolo? You want to take my son from me as the-price-of-the-honey? Do not joke with me like this." Yiriba said, "No, my younger brother, I am not joking. You have to give something. If you have no cowries, I will take Ngolo instead." Diara Dja was silent for a moment. It seemed almost as if the force of life had gone out of him. He said, "It is true. You are my older brother. You shelter me in your house. Everything I have you have given me. Everything I have is yours. My son is your son. He belongs to you. Therefore, if you insist, take your son and give him to the king. You will find him in the bush gathering firewood for his mother."

Yiriba went into the bush and found Ngolo. He did not allow Ngolo to return to the village to bathe and eat. He took him the way he was, in rags, and began the journey to Segu. Near the end of the day they came to the village of Sitki, and Yiriba lodged with the chief, named Dankala, as was the custom. After the two chiefs had exchanged news of their families and villages, Dankala asked the purpose of Yiriba's journey, and Yiriba said, "I am going to Segu to give the-price-of-the-honey to the king." Dankala asked, "Who is the small boy accompanying you?" Yiriba replied, "Aaah! He is the son of my brother, who didn't have cowries to pay his tax. So I am going to give the boy to the king." Dankala said, "Ééé! This is something I never heard of! No one has ever done such a thing before! My friend, listen to me. Take the boy home and leave him there. A boy cannot be used for taxes."

Yiriba said, "The reason I am taking him is that people are saying he will be a king. I don't want him in my village. Let him be a king-to-be somewhere else." Dankala replied, "Ééé! My friend, you are not smart. If you are blessed by having a king in your village, you want to throw him away? This is very strange." He tried to reason with Yiriba, but Yiriba would not listen. At last Dankala said, "Very well. Your mind is hard. But as for me, I want to demonstrate my respect for this boy. Perhaps some day he will remember it." Dankala had fresh clothes brought for Ngolo. He also gave him money and food to carry on the journey.

The next morning Yiriba and Ngolo continued on their way. They came to another village, called Kolokanda, whose chief was named Seriba. The two chiefs exchanged news of their families, and then Seriba asked questions about Ngolo. Yiriba explained that he was taking the boy to Segu to pay Diara Dja's tax. Seriba said, "Ah! What you are doing is not good! You are planting a bad seed. You may not live long enough to see it grow, but it will surely grow in the time of your children or grandchildren. If Ngolo truly becomes king, will he ever forget what you are doing today? Take him home now, before it is too late." But whatever Seriba said, Yiriba heard nothing.

The following day Yiriba and Ngolo went on toward Segu. In time they arrived at the town of Famuru, whose chief was Santakeba. Here it was the same as before, and Yiriba explained about Ngolo. He said, "People in my part of the country are saying that this boy will become king. I would like for your best filelikela or morike to examine him and tell me what he sees." So Santakeba sent for his most accomplished morike, a Muslim man of the mystic sciences, and asked him to say what he perceived about Ngolo. The morike scattered kolas on the ground and read them. After that he looked at

Ngolo a long while. Then he said, "Ééé! This boy will become king of Segu! You, Yiriba, are doing something very bad. You can do nothing to prevent him from becoming king. Therefore take him back to his village."

Yiriba said, "Haaah! I had some doubts about it, but what you tell me confirms everything. If he is going to be king, he will not live in my village but somewhere else." The morike tried to persuade Yiriba that he was doing a wrong thing. He said, "No one gives his brother's child away as a slave. If God gives you a king in your own family you should not throw him away." But Yiriba refused to listen. Santakeba, however, treated Ngolo with respect and gave him gifts. He said to Ngolo, "When you become king, remember me and look after my people."

After leaving Famuru, Yiriba and Ngolo went on until they reached Segu City, and the following morning they went to the king's court. When it was Yiriba's turn to be heard, he addressed himself to the king's chief djeli, named Sankoiba Koita, saying, "I have arrived from Niolla to bring the-price-of-the-honey from my village. I also bring respect to Biton Mamari from the counselors, the nobles, the blacksmiths, the slaves and the women of Niolla." Sankoiba Koita, the djeli, repeated to Biton Mamari in flourishing words what Yiriba had said. Biton Mamari answered, speaking through his djeli, "That is good." Yiriba handed the bag of cowries to the djeli, who gave it to the king's treasurer. Yiriba said, "The bag does not contain everything. My younger brother, Diara Dja, was unable to pay his tax in cowries. But I insisted that he would have to give something. Therefore I have brought his son, Ngolo, whom you see here, and I offer him to you in lieu of what Diara Dja should have paid."

The king said, "Aaah! Yes, I like him." Yiriba pushed the boy forward and continued to talk about the taxes. But Biton Mamari was turning over in his mind what had been said about Ngolo. He asked Yiriba to repeat his words. Yiriba said again, "This boy is the son of my younger brother, Diara Dja, who had no money to pay his tax. I present him to you in place of cowries." Biton Mamari pursued the matter. He said, "Ééé! Was it truly your own brother from whom you took the boy? Or was it only a distant relative?" Yiriba answered,

"No, he was my true brother. We had the same father, the same mother." The king said, "Aah, your own brother." Speaking through his djeli, Sankoiba Koita, he told Yiriba that he was free to leave, and Yiriba began his return journey to Niolla.

Biton Mamari ordered that Ngolo be taken into his household to perform whatever tasks were required of him. But never before had a child been given to him in place of cowries. He reflected. He spoke to his counselors about it. They said, "Everything belongs to the king. The gold of Segu, the cowries of Segu, the millet of Segu, the people of Segu, all belong to the king of Segu. Ngolo is yours to do with as you please." Yet Sankoiba Koita, the chief djeli, saw it differently. He said to Biton Mamari, "When a djeli says in his poem, 'All things belong to Biton Mamari,' that is a manner of speaking praise words. All the millet in the fields is yours, yet can you take away the people's millet and let them starve? All the gold is yours, yet can you confiscate it so that there is none left for the goldsmiths? All the cowries are yours, yet can you gather them all in your treasury and leave none for commerce in the marketplace? And all people are yours, but they are yours just as you are theirs. If a person is noble, a king can make him a slave. That is, the man can be made to serve as if he were a slave. Yet he is still noble. The brother of the chief of Niolla, though he is poor and sick, is still noble. Ngolo, though he has been traded for taxes, is still noble."

Biton Mamari reproached himself for having accepted Ngolo from Yiriba, not knowing how to deal with the boy. At first Ngolo was ordered about by everyone in the king's household, and he did whatever he was called on to do. Then one day the king's favorite wife, Baniaba, said to him, "Why don't you give Ngolo to me? He can serve in my house, and I can look after him." Biton Mamari said, "Yes, you can have him." So Baniaba took charge of Ngolo. He served in her house, and she treated him as a son.

However, the talk heard in the villages prophesying that Ngolo was destined to become king finally reached Segu. When it came to the attention of the morikes of the city, they consulted one another and performed divinations. After that they went to Biton Mamari and said, "Aaah, Master, you should know something that has been made known to us. Ngolo, the small boy you accepted as the-price-of-the-honey, has a destiny. When his time comes he will be the ruler of all Segu." Biton Mamari replied, "People say this and people say that. Perhaps it is nothing but marketplace gossip." The morikes said, "No, Master, we have performed divinations. What we tell you is true." Biton Mamari pondered. He said, "I have heard what you said. You have advised me that this poor boy from the bush will someday take power in Segu. Can it be proven?"

The senior morike said, "Let us carry out a test. If it goes one way, it will show that we are right. If it goes another way, it will show that we are wrong. Have food prepared in your kitchen. In the food we will place a nugget of gold. Invite all the children of the royal household to a feast—your own sons, the children of your counselors, the children of your servants and slaves. The food will be served in a large calabash, and each child will be given his portion in a gourd dish. We know by our divinations that whoever finds the gold nugget in his portion will be a future king of Segu." Biton Mamari said, "Very well, let us make the test." So food was prepared by the women, and the senior morike accepted a nugget of gold from the king and mixed it into the food. The children were brought together for the feast. And when the eating was finished, Biton Mamari asked, "You children, did any of you find something unusual in your food?" Ngolo replied, holding up the nugget, "Yes, I found gold in my gourd."

Biton Mamari now accepted the words of his morikes, and his spirit hardened against Ngolo. But Ngolo had not committed an offense for which he could be punished in any way. Biton Mamari thought, "I will help him to commit an offense." And he said aloud to Ngolo, "Thank you for finding my gold. Because you found it, I will let you keep it for me until I need it. A time will come when I will say, 'Ngolo, I need the piece of gold,' and then you will give it to me." Ngolo took the gold to the room where he slept. He tied it in a cloth, and he sewed the cloth inside his clothing.

After some days, the king sent for Ngolo and said to him, "Now I need the gold. You may give it to me." So Ngolo removed the gold from where he had secured it and gave it to Biton Mamari. The king had thought Ngolo would have lost the gold and thus committed an offense. When Ngolo produced the gold, however, Biton Mamari

31

handed it back, saying, "Oh, no, I do not really need it now after all. Keep it for me a while longer." Ngolo went away and again sewed the nugget safely inside his clothing.

Biton Mamari brooded. In his mind he saw Ngolo already presiding over the morning palace court, making great decisions and resolving disputes. He resolved to do whatever was necessary to dispose of Ngolo. And so one morning when he was sitting and watching his young sons playing together he said, "Now you are playing children's games, but it will not always be this way. For children grow into men, and men grow old and the light fades from their eyes. Yet the family goes on, and one Kulibali follows another. I also will come to my time, and then one of you will hold the power of kingship. That is the way it was intended to be. But now a young boy no older than you comes out of the bush and places a hand on the kingship. If Ngolo Diara continues to live, the kingship will pass out of the Kulibali family, and who knows what will happen to Segu?"

The children replied, "Father, you are king of everything. You own the people of Segu. You can order Ngolo to be killed." Biton Mamari said, "You do not understand. Even a king cannot behave that way. He can order an execution if someone commits treason or some other serious offense. It is said, 'Even a king cannot kill with a cold knife.' I gave Ngolo a piece of gold to keep for me. If he cannot return it when I ask for it, he will be guilty of a crime. But he has sewed the gold into a cloth and fastened it inside his clothing. There is no hope that he will lose it." And Biton Mamari's young sons replied, "Yes, Father, we understand. If the kingship should pass from the Kulibali family, we will not blame you." The king said, "Yes, I only wanted you to know my concerns."

That night the sons of the king went silently to the place where Ngolo was sleeping. They searched his clothing and found the cloth containing the gold, and they took it and carried it to the river and threw it into the water. After that they went to Biton Mamari's house and told him, "Father, you do not have to worry any longer about the gold." He answered. "Aaah! That is good."

Early the next morning the king sent for Ngolo and said, "Well, now, today I want the gold, so give it to me." Ngolo answered. "Last night someone came in the dark and took it from where it was hidden. I no longer have it." Biton Mamari said, "Ah, Ngolo! You have done a bad thing. I entrusted the gold to you and now you say you don't know where it is. It is a serious matter. If the gold is not returned to me by evening, you will be sacrificed to the Twelve Fetishes of Segu."

At last Biton Mamari had found an excuse to execute Ngolo. But it was a saying that no one can elude his destiny. He who is born to be a blacksmith will be a blacksmith. He who is born to be a hero will be a hero. He who is born to be a king will be a king. Ngolo went to Baniaba, who had cared for him as if he were her own child, and said, "Mother, the gold has been stolen from me and the king intends to kill me for it." Baniaba said, "Wait here for me," and she went immediately to the house of a certain woman who knew the art of divining with sand. The woman divined, and she said to Baniaba, "The sand speaks, but I cannot tell you the meaning of what it says. It instructs you to go to the river to take care of your laundry."

Baniaba returned to her house. She called on her female household slave to gather all the clothing that had to be washed. She took Ngolo with her to the river and began to wash clothes. There was a fisherman nearby working with his net. When he recognized the king's favorite wife, he brought her a large carp which he had just caught, saying, "Here is a good fish. You can make soup for Biton Mamari." Baniaba thanked him, and when the laundering was done she and Ngolo returned home. She said to Ngolo, "Clean the fish for me," and he did so. When he opened the fish he found in its stomach the cloth packet containing the king's gold. Baniaba exclaimed, "Ééé! The sand did not lie! Who is born to be a king will be a king! This evening you will take the gold to Biton Mamari and give it to him. If he wants you to take care of it again, refuse him gently. Tell him that you are only a child and that you should not be a guardian of gold."

When the sky was darkening, Ngolo went to the king's house. He said to Biton Mamari, "I have come to bring you the gold." The king said in surprise, "Aaah! Where did you find it?" Ngolo answered, "In the stomach of a carp that was given to Baniaba to make soup for you." Biton Mamari was discouraged. He could not now sacrifice Ngolo to the Twelve Fetishes, and he felt it to be true that the boy had a destiny. Yet he did not give up. He said, "Ngolo, that is very good. I am glad that you found the gold, because I have confidence in you. But now, as it happens, I do not have a need for it. Here, take it and keep it for me." Ngolo said, "Master, I cannot take charge of it any longer. You are a king and I am a small child. A king should not make a small boy his treasurer. The responsibility is too great."

Biton Mamari became angry. He said, "You refuse to do what the king of Segu tells you to do? That is a very great offense." But the king's djeli, Sankoiba Koita, spoke to Biton Mamari softly, saying, "Great king, you who resemble the sun, you who have everything, you whose name is heard everywhere, it is always an offense to say no to the ruler of Segu. But as the person is small, is not his offense small? There is a saying, 'Let the large canoe carry the heavy load, let the small canoe carry the lighter load.' Ngolo is still a young boy. His load should be a young boy's load. To be guardian of gold belonging to Biton Mamari is too heavy a thing for him. He refuses you only because he does not want to disappoint you if he fails. Your own sons, have they not sometimes said no when you have asked them for something? You are father to all the people of Segu. Therefore, although Ngolo has offended you, it was in a small way. Forgive him as you would your own children, so that in the future every djeli may call you the compassionate king." Biton Mamari could not deny what Sankoiba Koita had spoken so gently. He said to Ngolo, "Yes, the king forgives."

However, Biton Mamari was disturbed that Ngolo would go on living in Segu City, and he contrived a plan to send him away. He went to Baniaba and said to her, "You have always been my favorite wife. We have always shared things. You are the only wife I trust, and sometimes you have been my secret counselor. Let us consider this matter together. My sons are your sons. One of them ought to become king of Segu when I die. Yet it is said everywhere that Ngolo was born with a destiny. If we do not do something it is he who will become king of Segu. I cannot kill him with a cold knife. Therefore I must send him to a distant place. If he is not here in my city, perhaps his destiny will bend. I gave Ngolo to you. Now I ask you to give him back, and in exchange I will give you thirty slaves." Baniaba said to the king, "My husband, because I am a woman I have no choice but to do as you ask, even though I love Ngolo as if he were my own child. But one thing I know, his destiny will not bend no matter what you do."

Biton Mamari put Ngolo in the custody of his emissary, Suma Buare, saying, "Take the boy to Timbuktu and give him, as a gift from me, to the great morike Seku Mochtar Kadiri." Suma Buare and Ngolo made the long journey north to Timbuktu, traveling along the River Joliba. When they arrived in that city they went to the house of the great morike, and Suma Buare presented Ngolo as a present from the king of Segu. He said, "Biton Mamari gave much thought to what he might send you as a token of his respect. Biton Mamari said, 'I must give Seku Mochtar Kadiri something that I myself value. Therefore I will give him Ngolo Diara.' Now I have brought Ngolo Diara to you to use in whatever manner you see fit."

When the great morike looked at Ngolo he said, "Aaah!" For his command of the Muslim mystic sciences gave him the power to see what others could not. He said nothing about what he saw, and behaved as though he were accepting the gift. He ordered one of his slaves to provide food and a place for Ngolo to sleep. To Suma Buare he said, "Come back to see me before you return to Segu," and Suma Buare agreed to do so.

The next day Seku Mochtar Kadiri sent for Ngolo to come and talk with him. He said, "Ngolo, I saw you in the night while you were sleeping. Light radiated from your body in the darkness. I know that one day you will be king of Segu. I know that you have been mistreated, and that when you have the power to do it you will avenge yourself on this family or that family. I refuse to accept you as a slave given by Biton Mamari. Tell me, now, what you will do for me when you have Segu in your hand." Ngolo said, "Great master of the mystic sciences, when I become king of Segu I will send you a large measure of gold, thirty slaves, one hundred cows, one hundred sheep and one hundred chickens every year." Seku Mochtar Kadiri replied, "Yes, that is good. But what I want above all is to be appointed the paramount morike of Segu, and I also want your pledge that you will protect my children and grandchildren from any harm as long as you rule." Ngolo said, "Great morike, yes, I pledge all this."

Seku Mochtar Kadiri took pen and ink and wrote some mystical words on a heavy rock. When the ink dried, the morike placed the rock on Ngolo's head, saying, "Carry this rock, step by step, as far as you can. Do not hesitate, do not falter, and count your steps as you go." Ngolo did as he was instructed. He walked, counting his steps aloud. After his tenth step he could not go any farther, and he placed the rock on the ground. Seku Mochtar Kadiri said, "The number is ten, meaning that there will be ten kings in your line, yourself and nine others. This is what has been revealed to us, and it will be written in the history of Segu."

After that, the great morike sent for Biton Mamari's emissary, Suma Buare, and asked him, "When are you returning to Segu?" Suma Buare said, "I will begin the journey tomorrow." Seku Mochtar Kadiri said, "That is good, but please return as you came, in the company of Ngolo Diara. Tell Biton Mamari that I thank him for his gift, but that I cannot accept Ngolo. Tell Biton Mamari that Ngolo radiates light in the darkness of night. There is no way to avoid what is coming. Destiny winds like a river, it seems to go one way and another, but it begins at the beginning and ends at the end."

So Suma Buare and Ngolo returned together to Segu. And while they were still on the journey, Suma Buare, like the great morike of Timbuktu, sought a pledge from Ngolo, saying, "Ngolo Diara, I have taken care of you on this journey and shown you respect. Promise me that when you become king of Segu you will do nothing to harm my family." Ngolo answered, "Yes, I pledge it. If your children or grandchildren need help, I will help them."

When they arrived in Segu City they went to the king's court. Seeing Ngolo standing there with his emissary, the king said in surprise, "Aaah!" And Suma Buare said, "Great king, I took the boy to Timbuktu as you instructed me to do. I brought him safely to Seku Mochtar Kadiri. With great respect I offered him to Seku Mochtar Kadiri as a gift from you. But he declined to accept your gift. He looked at Ngolo, he said that Ngolo radiates light in the darkness. He said, 'One cannot deflect destiny. No matter how a river winds, it begins at the beginning and ends at the end.'" Biton Mamari exclaimed, "Aaah!" once more. And after Ngolo went to the house of Baniaba to sleep, Biton Mamari said, "What can I do now? This Ngolo plagues me. Is there no way to separate him from Segu? He clings to me like a fly caught in pitch."

Some years passed. Ngolo Diara grew up in the household of the king. He became a young man. Whenever Biton Mamari saw him he turned his face away, denying Ngolo's existence. And as Ngolo grew older, the king's mind grew more troubled, for the water in the river was flowing toward the end. Then, one night, it came to Biton Mamari that he might rid himself of Ngolo by making him a tax collector at a station on a distant road that ran through a wild part of the bush. Perhaps Ngolo would be killed by violent men seeking to appropriate the king's cowries, for there were other tax collectors who had gone to their stations and never returned.

So Ngolo was appointed tax collector, and he went to a distant place in the bush and built a hut for himself overlooking a road along which many traders traveled. There he collected highway taxes, and once a year he returned to Segu to deliver the cowries to the king's treasurer.

Not far from Ngolo's station was a small village, and there was a young man there, Sumana Djire, with whom he became friends. One day when the two of them were together, Ngolo said, "I am lonesome living at the tax station by myself." Sumana said, "Yes, you need a wife." Ngolo replied, "I have thought of it. But I have no family to speak for me." Sumana said, "You do have a family. We will ask my father to speak for you."

They went to Sumana's father, whose name was Suri Burama Djire, and spoke to him about getting a wife for Ngolo. Suri Burama Djire said, "Because you and my son are friends, I will consider you a son and do what I can." He suggested one young woman and another, but Ngolo declined them all. At last Suri Burama Djire said, "You, friend of my son, want a wife but all you can say is no. Whom, then, do you want?" Ngolo answered, "My elder friend, you who will speak for me as a father, the one I want for a wife is Nakurni, a daughter of Biton Mamari Kulibali. Many young men want this girl, but they are afraid to ask the king for her. If you hesitate to speak with the king about this, I will understand." Suri Burama Djire said, "Ngolo, my family is just as noble as Biton

Mamari's. Why should I be afraid to speak to him? To say the word *fire* will not burn your mouth. Do not be concerned about it. I will ask Biton Mamari to give his daughter to you."

He went to the capital city and spoke first with the king's first djeli, Sankoiba Koita, telling him the purpose of his visit. He said, "Ngolo has been buffeted by fate since he was a child. But he is honest and loyal, and he is descended from a noble line." Sankoiba Koita answered, "Yes, it is so. Biton Mamari is not more noble than Ngolo. And the king knows that Ngolo has a destiny. Let us speak with him." They went to Biton Mamari and the djeli informed him why Suri Burama Djire had come. When the king had heard everything, he thought, "Now the river approaches its end." Both Suri Burama Djire and the djeli expected Biton Mamari to grow hot with anger, but he did not. He spoke with resignation, saying, "Ééé! I know now that there is no magic strong enough to deflect destiny. Because Ngolo will some day become king of Segu, I will give him my daughter. I only ask him to pledge that when that time comes he will treat my descendents with honor and respect."

So it was that Ngolo Diara, who had been given to Biton Mamari Kulibali as the-price-of-the-honey, received the king's daughter as his wife. He lived on. He took his place in the life of Segu, and was accepted into the Tonjon, the army of nobles created by Biton Mamari. He was a friend of the three djelis of the king's court— Sankoiba Koita, Mamui Kone and Ngoroni Jabate. He had children. He gained respect and honor.

Biton Mamari grew old, and a day came when the light faded for him. He was the first of Segu's true kings, and even though some of his personal actions were not worthy, in a large way he governed Segu well. Though he feared conspiracy on the part of Ngolo Diara, Ngolo never conspired against him. And when Biton Mamari died, Ngolo did nothing at all to interfere with the family succession. There was a saying, "One may travel to Timbuktu in the night without seeing anything." It meant that although an outcome might be foretold in a prophecy, the chain of events leading to the outcome might not be foreseen. Biton Mamari feared that when he died his place would be taken over by Ngolo. But although the kola nuts of the morikes still told that Ngolo would be king, it was not he but Biton Mamari's eldest son Chekoro who was put into power. And when Chekoro died, another son of Biton Mamari, named Dankoro, became king.

Dankoro was a leper. Whether his illness affected his character cannot be said, but he was ruthless in the use of his authority, and he frequently did things far in excess of what was natural. Nothing could be done to alter his behavior. Counselors who tried to temper his ways were severely punished. One day he demonstrated that there were no limits to his power by executing four hundred forty officers of the Tonjon because, he said, they were not sufficiently loyal. When this happened, other leaders in the Tonjon met in secret and decided that Dankoro must be killed.

That night two men scaled the wall surrounding the king's compound and made their way into his sleeping room. They put a twisted cloth around his neck and tightened it. He could not make a sound. Though his voice was not audible, his silent words were, "I leave this place to you." In this way King Dankoro died. The following morning when it was time for him to come out and meet with his officials and counselors, Dankoro did not appear. The people waited. They said, "Aaah! Is something wrong?" A delegation was sent to the king's room. They returned. They said, "The king has lost his key," meaning that he was no longer alive. The funeral was arranged. Dankoro was buried.

Now, other sons of Biton Mamari Kulibali were still living, but the tonjons decided to take over power, and they named their senior member to become king. His name was Ton Mansa. He ruled. Segu went on, still a great kingdom.

Ton Mansa had many wives, but none of them had given him a child. He consulted the morikes and the filelikelas of Segu, but they were unable to do anything for him. Ton Mansa brooded. He wanted his name to be carried on from generation to generation. At last he called a meeting of one hundred morikes. He told them, "I have something for you to do. I want you to make me immortal. If you succeed, I will give you gold, cattle, sheep, slaves, land and honors. But if you fail, I will excute you and sacrifice your blood to the Twelve Fetishes of Segu." The morikes said, "Eh! Great king, this is an impossible thing." Ton Mansa replied, "If you do not do it you will die."

The morikes met in another place and discussed their problem.

They did not know what to do. So they decided to send a delegation to Timbuktu to consult the great Seku Mochtar Kadiri. The delegation made the journey. They went to Seku Mochtar Kadiri and told him their story. They said, "Ton Mansa will kill us if we do not make him immortal. But only Allah is immortal. Tell us what to do."

Seku Mochtar Kadiri said, "Before you can do anything, you must understand. You morikes have studied the mysteries of the Koran. That is good. But to be great in your profession you must also study the mysteries of a man's mind. The simplest things escape you. When Ton Mansa says he wants to be immortal, he does not mean that he wants his body to live forever. He knows that all men die. But he has no son to carry on for him and make his name remembered. Therefore he wants you to do something so that future generations will say, 'Once there was Ton Mansa.' That is the only immortality there is for him." The morikes from Segu said, "Aaah! Great Master, you have taught us something. Thank you." They returned to Segu and reported what they had learned, and they also told the king that they were ready to do their work.

The one hundred morikes of Segu convened a secret meeting from which they did not emerge for several days. After that, they employed workers to dig a large well for them. They went to Ton Mansa and said, "We are making a large well, and in it we are going to place one hundred frogs. These frogs will sing your name and praise you generation after generation, so that no one will forget that you have been king of Segu." Ton Mansa answered, "Yes, this is what I want." When the digging of the well was completed, the morikes had one hundred frogs gathered for them, and with magic ink they wrote mystical words on the tongues of the frogs. The frogs were placed in the well and it was covered with a lid made of gold, and the gold lid was fastened with a silver chain. The morikes told Ton Mansa, "Tomorrow evening the frogs will begin singing your praises."

The next evening the people of Segu heard praise songs for Ton Mansa coming from the well. They heard not the coarse croaking voices of frogs, but melodious human voices singing:

Who in life is equal to Ton Mansa?
He is master of the Tonjon,
He is the king of all Segu,
King of the land and the river,
All things are his.
Ton Mansa rules, but he is just.
Ton Mansa is rich, but he is generous.

It is said that in the times that followed, if a man heard the frogs singing in the night he would awaken his wife to listen, for if he did not do so she would be angry and hold it against him. The praise songs the frogs sang about Ton Mansa were learned by the djelis of Segu and passed on to later generations.

When his time came, Ton Mansa died, and the Tonjon elected another of their men to become king; and when he in his turn died they elected another. Several Tonjon kings ruled Segu. Then at last Ngolo Diara claimed the right to govern. Among the tonjons there was disagreement and dissension. Some asserted that the most senior person in the army should be given the right to rule, and they supported a particular man. But Ngolo proved that he himself had lived in Segu a longer time, and was therefore senior to the other man. In the end the tonjons accepted him. They said, "Ngolo Diara, we name you to the kingship. You will not do harm to anyone, and no one will do harm to you." Ngolo answered, "Yes, I agree."

Ngolo had a son named Bamudje, already a young man, and at the time the Tonjon appointed Ngolo, Bamudje was returning with a group of fighters from a small military expedition. When he arrived in Segu he said to his father, "The Tonjon gives and the Tonjon takes, according to its urges. What were the oaths that were sworn to?" Ngolo replied, "It was said, 'Ngolo, you will not do harm to anyone, and no one will do harm to you.'" Bamudje said, "Ah, my father, it was no pledge at all. You are king of Segu, and the Tonjon is an organization of slaves. All they told you was, 'Be careful what you do.' A father teaches his child, yet sometimes a child can speak wisdom. I will see to it that the proper pledges are given by the

41

Tonjon. Now you must make it known in Segu that appropriate sacrifices will be made to the Twelve Fetishes in twenty-one days. Call on all of the tonjons to be present for the ceremony. Tell them that they are to come without weapons." Ngolo made the announcement.

Bamudje, his son, mounted his horse and rode away to the city of Saudugu to gather an army. The day of the sacrifice arrived, and the men of the Tonjon gathered outside the city without weapons. One hundred cows were killed, one hundred goats, one hundred sheep, one hundred of everything. The tonjons sat feasting and drinking wine. And while they were occupied in this way, Bamudje arrived with his army from Saudugu. He encircled the tonjons with his army. Then he addressed the crowd, saying, "Segu, on what terms have you made my father king?" They answered, "You will not do harm to anyone, and no one will do harm to you." Bamudje said, "Ééé! I did not hear it." They repeated, "You will not do harm to anyone, and no one will do harm to you." Bamudje said, "Ééé! Tell me once more." The tonjons called back, "You will not do harm to anyone, and no one will do harm to you."

Bamudje asked his father to come out of the crowd and stand beside him. Ngolo did so, and Bamudje said to the feasting tonjons, "You tonjons, whoever created you equal to the king of Segu? You are his slaves. How dare you say to him. 'Do nothing bad to us and we will do nothing bad to you'?" Bamudje ordered his soldiers to open fire, and they killed many of the tonjons. The tonjons called out, "Bamudje, stop the firing. We have something to say." Bamudje ordered the shooting to stop. A leader of the tonjons said, "Yes, yes, you are right. The swearing was wrong. Forgive us. This is the way it is to be: Ngolo Diara is our king, and we are his club of slaves. Ngolo does what he wishes. Whatever he wants us to do, we will do it. Segu is his kingdom, and it is he alone who will appoint his heir."

Bamudje called out, "All of Segu is here. All of Segu has heard the pledge of the Tonjon. You are witnesses to what has been said. Did you hear it clearly?" And the crowd called back, "Yes, we have heard it." Bamudje said, "You people of Segu, swear with wine that you have heard the pledge." The people drank wine to affirm that they had heard the pledge of the Tonjon.

In this way Ngolo Diara's kingship was confirmed and the power of the Tonjon ended. Segu was Ngolo's alone to rule. It remained strong and united for many years. When at last Ngolo died, his son became king, and after that other sons of the family of Diara. Under the Diaras, Segu flourished and became greater still.

BASSADJALAN ZAMBELE AND THE HEROES OF KALA

BASSADJALAN ZAMBELE WAS A HERO of Segu. He lived and he died. Yet who he was and what he achieved are remembered by the djeli, who sing:

Bassadjalan Zambele.
Zambele from Bassadjalan,
He appeared, he disappeared,
He lived out his time
But he is not forgotten.
His name is written in golden ink
In the story of Segu.

When Bassadjalan Zambele was young he said to his father, "I want to go to a faraway place and prove my valor." His father answered, "Not yet. You are not ready. You are not armed for what you want to do." Bassadjalan Zambele said, "My father, I am armed with a spear and a gun and my courage." His father said, "It is true, yet you are only half armed. All who do great deeds have such things, but they must also have the power of medicine. It is courage that guides a man into combat, but it is mystic medicine that protects him from the bullets of his enemies and makes his own bullets fly true."

Bassadjalan Zambele's father was accomplished in the mystic sciences. He went into the bush to collect roots, leaves and herbs, and from these things he prepared powders and lotions. Every day he rubbed the lotions on his son's body. He made cuts in Bassadjalan's skin and applied mystic powders to the cuts. He made talismans for Bassadjalan to wear.

Time passed, and Bassadjalan asked his father, "Am I not ready?" His father replied, "Not yet." Then one day his father said, "My son, walk toward that tree over there without looking back." Bassadjalan did what his father instructed him to do. His father picked up his gun and fired at Bassadjalan. The powder fizzled but did not explode, and the bullet merely fell from the mouth of the barrel. Bassadjalan's father said, "My son, it seems that you are now ready. Bullets cannot harm you. There is one more thing. I have made this magic garan for you. It appears to be of ordinary rope. But do not think it should be used for hobbling your horse. It is a powerful weapon. Use it against your enemy when you wish to subdue him without killing him. Your enemy will feel pain, cry out, and become helpless. I cannot do anything more to prepare you. But there is something for you to remember. Other men also have been prepared. Whenever you meet someone in conflict, do not forget that he too is protected by the powers of mystic medicine. Courage fights courage, strength fights strength, but only medicine can fight medicine."

So at last Bassadjalan Zambele began his journey into the world accompanied by a personal slave. He rode through many villages, rested, and went on. He journeyed for many days. In time he came to a town called Kala. He inquired if there was a house in Kala where he could lodge. A woman directed him to a certain place, saying, "In that house two women are living. They have lost their husbands, and perhaps they will have a space in which you can sleep." He went there. He spoke to the two women. They sent for a male relative to come, and he asked Bassadjalan questions, saying, "My brother, you are welcome. But who are you and why are you here?" Bassadjalan answered, "My name is Zambele and I come from Bassadjalan, therefore I am called Bassadjalan Zambele. I lived in my village. I departed from there to find knowledge and accomplish valorous deeds. That is why I am here." The man said, "Aaah! Yes, Kala is a place where heroes live. There are brave men here. But we must know, do you come as a child or as a man?" Bassadjalan took offense, but he replied gently, "When I was young and in the care of my mother I was a child. But I did not die in my childhood. I became a man. Even if I wished it, I could not be a child again. Because I am a man I came to Kala." His questioner said, "Good. You have a place to sleep. But in Kala the heroes spend their waking hours with heroes. The women spend their time with women." Bassadjalan Zambele said, "Yes, I hear what you are saying."

But Bassadjalan liked the company of the two women, and he sat with them for long hours conversing. He told them about life in other places, and they told him about life in Kala. He did not go and sit with the men on the terrace where they met, boasted of their accomplishments and drank wine. The two women had six brothers. One of them said, "Aaah! This fellow who has arrived in Kala, is he a man or a woman? He only sits and gossips with my sisters. Why is he not here on the terrace reserved for valorous men? He has contempt for us. We should invite him to join us and give him wine. When he has drunk enough wine he may say something offensive and then we can deal with him."

The next day the brothers had wine brought to the terrace and sent a messenger to Bassadjalan inviting him to join them. Bassadjalan declined the invitation, saying, "No, I cannot drink with you like this. There is nothing between us to make us feel close. All I have in common with you is that your sisters allow me to sleep in their house. I do not know enough about you, and if we were to drink together I might say something to offend someone. When a man is drunk he cannot control his thoughts or his words. His tongue runs away with him."

On hearing this answer, the heroes became disconcerted. They thought, "If he does not join us and do something offensive, how can we punish him?" Someone said, "Let us do it this way. Tomorrow we will kill the Cow of Heroes, and each hero will take the portion that is his. We will invite Bassadjalan to come. If he refuses to come, it will mean that he is too cowardly to make a claim on the meat. Then we will throw him out of the town. If he comes, we will see if he is courageous enough to claim a portion." So they sent another message to Bassadjalan Zambele to come the next day to where the Cow of Heroes would be divided. Now, every portion of the meat had a particular meaning, and the two women who were caring for Bassadjalan were worried that he would claim something that would cause trouble. They said to him, "When you go there, be careful what you say. Do not provoke anyone. And be careful, if you claim anything at all, to claim modestly. The heroes are looking for an excuse to kill you."

The next day Bassadjalan and his slave went to the place where the Cow of Heroes had been butchered. All the parts had been laid out on the grass. The six brothers and the other heroes of Kala were waiting. The eldest of the brothers said, "So you have arrived. We did not know whether you would come, because we are not sure whether you are a boy or a man. But you let it be known that you came to Kala looking for honor. Therefore we invited you. Take your portion."

Bassadjalan went to where the meat was laid out. He put his foot on the head of the cow, saying to his slave, "Take the cow's head, because I, Bassadjalan Zambele, am the head of everything. If war comes, I will be the leader." His slave took the head and set it aside. Bassadjalan Zambele then placed his foot on the cow's chest, saying to his slave, "Take the chest. If war comes I will be the main substance and the heart of Kala." His slave picked up the chest and set it aside. After that Bassadjalan Zambele placed his foot on the cow's right foreleg, saying to his slave, "Take the right foreleg. If war comes, I will be foremost in battle." To the assembled heroes Bassadjalan said, "You men can have what remains of the meat. I, Bassadjalan, claim the noblest parts because I will be the commander, the strength and the foremost in war." His slave took up the three noble portions and carried them away.

After Bassadjalan departed, the brothers were very angry. "This boy has insulted us. He tells us he is the leader. He tells us he is the power. He tells us he is the foremost. It is hard to believe that we heard it. Now it is clear that something must be done to deal with him." Bassadjalan's slave brought the meat to the house and gave it to the two sisters. Bassadjalan said to the women, "Prepare the meat for me. I took the head because I will be the leader, the chest because I am the strongest and the foreleg because I will be first." The women exclaimed, "Ééé! You have been brash, Bassadjalan. You have given them the provocation they were waiting for. Now, because you have boasted that you surpass them in every way, they will kill you." Bassadjalan soothed them, saying, "No, do not be concerned. What I said was true. They cannot harm me."

The brothers discussed how they might humiliate and destroy Bassadjalan. They conspired against him. They came to where he was living and told him, "Be ready the day after tomorrow. We are going to fight against the town of Koble, whose chief is Zanke." Bassadjalan said, "Yes, do not think any more about it. I will be ready." The two women understood what was happening, and they sought out their six brothers and said, "What you are planning to do is not honorable. It is Bassadjalan you want to destroy, not the town of Koble. For many years you have tried to defeat Zanke without succeeding. Now you hope to make Bassadjalan face Zanke and his twelve sons. You hope to make him face Ntchi, Zanke's giant future son-in-law. Ntchi is twice the size of an ordinary man. His strength is that of two hundred ordinary heroes. His war knife is equal to fifty ordinary knives." The six brothers answered, "Bassadjalan proclaims himself to be the greatest of everything. Now let him prove that he is the head, the chest and the right foreleg."

The two women warned Bassadjalan. He said, "Yes, I understand what they want to do to me. But they will not be able to do it." He went to the numuke of the town who forged weapons for the heroes. He asked the numuke to make a weapon for him and endow it with mystic powers. It was a stick of wood with a knob at each end, to be covered with silver. The numuke understood how to make this weapon. He said, "Come back tomorrow." When Bassadjalan returned the next day the weapon was finished and covered with silver. The numuke said, "This weapon is more powerful than any spear or gun in Kala." Bassadjalan tried to give the numuke something for his work, but the man said to him, "No, I cannot accept cowries or gold for this work. Though you are a stranger here I can see that you are a good man and a noble. I can also see that the heroes of the town are conspiring against you. I am giving you this weapon for the sake of honor."

Bassadjalan replied, "Yes, let it be that way. I am going to fight against Zanke of Koble. When I return I will bring all his cattle, and you will choose the best of them in exchange for your work." The numuke said, "Ééé, my master! You are saying something great. To say something great is easy, but to accomplish something great is hard. Zanke has two hundred valiant fighting men who are hunters in time of peace. In time of war they are formidable fighters. He has twelve sons, each of them a proven hero in his own right. He has the giant Ntchi, his future son-in-law to whom his daughter Nyiba is pledged. Your enterprise will be difficult."

When he returned to his house, the two sisters urged him, "Bassadjalan, do not go on the expedition. It is only a conspiracy to humiliate you. If you ever get to Koble you will not come back alive. Your head will remain there as a trophy." Bassadjalan answered, "Do not be concerned. I will come back, and I will bring Zanke's daughter Nyiba and the giant Ntchi with me as slaves."

The following morning the brothers came to get Bassadjalan. He was still sleeping. They awakened him, saying, "Bassadjalan, when you go to war you must begin the expedition before daylight. We see now that you are really a woman who knows nothing about such things. We cannot wait. We are going ahead." They departed on their horses. Bassadjalan then arose and dressed. The women gave him food. He mounted his horse, saying to his slave, "Let us go now to find out what is happening at Koble."

The six brothers rode toward Koble. Still early in the day they were in sight of its walls. The town was nearly empty of men, because the farmers were in the fields and the hunters were in the bush. The brothers stopped where they were and fired their guns in the air, creating the sounds of battle, and after that they turned and rode back toward Kala. On the way they met Bassadjalan Zambele coming on his horse. They taunted him, saying, "Aaah! You who are the strongest of all and the first in everything, finally you arrive. Koble is waiting for you. We ourselves did not come to make war against anybody, only to let you prove you are the head, the chest and the right foreleg." Having spoken this way, they went on toward Kala.

Bassadjalan rode forward into the town of Koble. He went to the house of the chief, Zanke, and at the gate he shouted, "You with the great name Zanke, come and welcome me." Zanke came out and asked, "Who are you?" Bassadjalan answered, "I am Bassadjalan Zambele, and I have come to take your four hundred cattle, and also to make slaves of your daughter Nyiba and the giant called Ntchi." Zanke replied, "Young brother, where is your army?" Bassadjalan said, "I am the head, the chest and the right foreleg, and I am the army as well." Zanke answered, "Very well, you are welcome to my town. Wait until I clothe myself properly to receive you." Zanke prepared himself. He put on his battle shirt, his war cap and his talismans. He picked up his weapons and mounted his horse. He came riding. He fired his gun at Bassadjalan, but his powder only fizzled and the bullet fell from the mouth of the barrel. Three times his gun misfired. His slave handed him his spear. Zanke rode forward to attack with his spear, but Bassadjalan evaded the thrust and struck Zanke with the silver-covered weapon that the numuke of Kala had made for him. Zanke fell from his horse and lay on the ground. The breath had gone out of his body.

Bassadjalan asked Zanke's slave, "Where is the house of Zanke's daughter Nyiba?" The slave pointed it out. Bassadjalan went there and said to her, "Your father is dead. I am taking you as a slave to Kala." He led her outside the town walls and ordered her to sit on the ground. He said, "I have been here a long time, but it would not be honorable for me to take you without your twelve brothers and your fiancé having a chance to prevent it." She answered, "Yes, they are surely coming."

The fields where the men of Koble were working were some distance from the town. When they heard gunfire, the eldest son of Zanke sent his youngest brother to find out what was happening. As the youngest brother approached the town walls, an old man on a rooftop called out, "Be careful. A warrior came on a horse. He killed your father and took your sister as a slave. He is out there waiting for you." The youngest son went to where Bassadjalan was waiting. They fought. Bassadjalan struck him with his silver-covered fighting stick and killed him.

When the youngest brother did not come back, the next youngest was sent. Everything was the same as before. He fought with Bassadjalan and died. The next youngest came to see what had happened, and he also died. One by one the girl's brothers came and

Bassadjalan defeated them all. He said to Nyiba, "Now let us go. You see how it is. Your family fought honorably but they could not win your freedom. Let us find your fiancé, Ntchi, for I pledged to bring him back to Kala." She said, "Wait, he will come."

What Nyiba said was true. Ntchi came riding from the west. He was far taller than any man Bassadjalan had ever seen, and his horse was very large but fleet. Ntchi's breast and arms were covered by a hundred amulets that undulated with the stride of his horse. A band of gold and silver talismans was on his forehead. His stirrups were of silver. The horse had feathered amulets woven into his forelock and his tail. The western sun behind Ntchi's back made him appear even larger than he was, and his shadow on the ground was the length of ten ordinary men. He halted his horse at a distance and sat looking at Bassadjalan and Nyiba.

Bassadjalan said, "Welcome, hero of Koble. I have been waiting for you." And Ntchi answered, "I hear you, Bassadjalan. You have something that belongs to me. You have performed some notable deeds today. Yet, what were they? How will the djeli sing of you? They will say you killed Zanke, who was an old man. They will say you killed his sons, who were children. They will say you stole a young girl who could not fight back. You know who I am. My praise name is Two Hundred Men. The praise name of my knife is Fifty Knives. You are young, and until today you were not known anywhere. Perhaps you are not even noble, who can say? Since you came from nowhere, return to nowhere and leave the girl where she is. For me to kill you would not add anything to the luster I already have. Come back another day when you have earned the right to be called a hero, then I will fight you."

Bassadjalan answered, "You whose praise name is Two Hundred Men, be assured that I am a noble. My father was a hero ad his father was a hero. To hear a name, there is always a first time. Today you heard it and addressed me as Bassadjalan. That is good. For who wants to be defeated in battle by someone whose name he does not know? Though you are great in size, and though you wear your amulets with pride, you speak gently and in an honorable way. If I could be your friend I would gladly do it. If I could leave the girl and go away I would gladly do it. But I have to fight you because I am pledged to it. Now that we have welcomed each other, let us begin."

The two horsemen rode at each other, striking out with their weapons. Ntchi slashed with his sword and Bassadjalan Zambele struck with his silver stick. Their horses wheeled, rode apart, and came back together again. They fought a long time, and the dust they stirred up rose and hung like a cloud in the sky. At last Bassadjalan's silver weapon struck the sword from Ntchi's grasp and it fell to the ground. But Ntchi grasped Bassadjalan's weapon and wrenched it away from him. In doing so he lost his balance and fell from his horse, but he could not disentangle one foot from its stirrup and he was dragged on the ground. Bassadjalan dismounted. He struck Ntchi with the magic garan his father had made for him. Ntchi became helpless. He could not fight anymore. He said, "It is over. Take my head." Bassadjalan said, "No, I cannot do it. I am pledged to take you and Nyiba back to Kala as slaves." He tied Ntchi's hands behind him, and the other end of the rope he gave to Nyiba to hold, saying, "Now let us go."

They went then to the place where Zanke's four hundred cattle were kept. Bassadjalan said to the Fula who guarded them, "I have killed Zanke and his twelve sons. As you see, Ntchi and Nyiba are my slaves. The cattle are mine and you are my herdsman. Take the cattle to Kala." The Fula did as he was told. They began the journey through the bush.

Zanke's two hundred hunter-fighters had been looking for game at a distant place. They saw dust rising in the air as if a great herd of cattle was moving. The chief hunter said, "Something unusual is happening." They went closer. They saw Bassadjalan riding, followed by his slave, the girl Nyiba, the tall warrior Ntchi and the Fula herdsman driving Zanke's cattle. The chief hunter said, "What we see tells us that our town has been conquered. Yet I see no army, only a single man riding a horse. He must have great mystic strength. Therefore let us be cautious. Wait here. I will go alone to talk to him."

The chief hunter rode out of the bush to meet Bassadjalan. He said, "You who lead captives and cattle from my town, what kind of man are you? I am the chief of Zanke's hunters. Relinquish your booty immediately, otherwise I will have to kill you." Bassadjalan answered, "Aaah, you do not understand the story. I am Zambele from Bassadjalan. I came to this country looking for honor. I went alone to your town. I killed Zanke and his twelve sons. I took Ntchi and Nyiba as slaves. I took Zanke's four hundred cows. Everything was done with honor, so you see I did not steal anything. You, chief hunter, you are an old man the age of my father and I do not want to humiliate you. Let us not fight. Go back to your hunting and I will go on to Kala."

The chief hunter said, "No, I cannot let you pass. My responsibility is to protect Zanke's town. You will have to fight." So Bassadjalan ordered his slave to proceed to Kala with the captives, and he ordered the Fula herdsman to follow with the cattle. Then he said to the chief hunter, "My father, are you ready?" The chief hunter said, "I am ready." Bassadjalan said, "Hunter, this is the way it will be. Load your gun and prepare to shoot. I will start at that rock over there. I will ride slowly toward you. When you are ready, shoot. If you kill me you may reclaim the captives and the cattle and take them back to Koble." The chief hunter said, "I hear you." Bassadjalan rode to the rock, turned and came back. The chief hunter pulled his trigger. The powder did not explode, it merely fizzled and the bullet fell harmlessly from the barrel.

Bassadjalan placed one foot on the chief hunter's head, saying, "You see, it is better to let things be as they are. I do not want to kill a man the age of my father." But the chief hunter said, "I realize now that I was not ready. I did not appeal to my talismans. I did not have anything to offer them." Bassadjalan said, "Very well, you may do it. What is it you need to offer them?" The chief hunter replied, "Two red kola nuts." Bassadjalan took two red kolas from his bag and gave them to the man, who retired a little distance and made his offering. He returned. He said, "Now I am ready." Bassadjalan again rode to the rock and came back. Again the chief hunter pulled his trigger, but once more the powder only fizzled. Bassadjalan said, "Give it up now, Father, it is useless." Yet the hunter persisted, saying, "No, not until I have made an offering to another talisman." Bassadjalan asked, "What is it you need for this one?" The man replied, "I need one red kola and two white kolas." Bassadjalan gave them to him, and the man retired a little and made his offering. After that they began again, Bassadjalan riding from the rock and the man pulling his trigger. But it was the same as before. His powder did not explode.

Bassadjalan said, "You tried three times. Therefore it is finished. Let me go now or I will be forced to kill you." The chief hunter said, "Bassadjalan, I know now that everything you told me is true. I can see that you are a noble man. I give myself to you as a slave." Bassadjalan answered, "No, you resemble my father. How could I accept you as a slave?" The chief hunter said, "I do not care what you call me, but I am the chief of two hundred men. We will follow you and do whatever you want us to do." Bassadjalan said, "Yes, that is good." So when he arrived at last in Kala he had two slaves, two hundred fighters and four hundred cattle.

He went first to the two sisters who had lodged him in their house. He said to them, "Everything you told me was true. Your brothers tried to destroy me. They left me to fight alone. I killed Zanke and his sons. I took all his cattle. I also took Zanke's daughter and the giant hero Ntchi as slaves and I give them to you as a gift." The sisters said, "Bassadjalan, you have proved your valor. We know what our brothers did. You have the right to punish them, but we beg you not to do it." Bassadjalan said, "Daughters of a noble father, you have been good to me. But how can I ignore what your brothers have done? They pledged themselves to fight honorably, and when they came to the walls of Koble they fired their guns in the air and turned back as if it did not matter. They forfeited their right to be treated generously." The sisters spoke earnestly, saying, "Bassadjalan, we beg you not to kill them. First we beg you because we are the only ones who showed you hospitality when you arrived here. We also beg you because we are women, and it is a saying that when a woman begs a man should listen. Again we beg you because of the infants we carry on our backs." Bassadjalan replied, "If your brothers had begged me I would not have been able to hear their voices. But because of you I promise not to hurt them."

After that Bassadjalan went to the numuke who had made his silver weapon for him. He said, "You, my numuke, I promised you a cow in payment. I have conquered Zanke and taken his cattle. Come and choose the cow you want for yourself." The numuke went with Bassadjalan and chose a cow from the herd. Bassadjalan said, "Take more," but the numuke refused, saying, "We spoke of one cow, no more. These were our words, and the words of men are the men themselves."

55

Bassadjalan said to the numuke, "Although I have not been in your town long, I can see already that Kala is afflicted by false heroes. I have pledged not to hurt the six brothers who enticed me to fight against all of Koble by myself. Tell me who is the greatest of the heroes in your town and I will challenge him." The numuke said, "Why, as everyone knows, the man named Didiya Tiekele is the greatest. He is feared by all the people. He is rich. He owns vast fields and has many slaves to cultivate for him. But his character is not good. He abuses ordinary people and makes them do things for him as if they were slaves. When harvest time comes, he sends his djeli to the four gates of Kala to notify the people to go to his fields and bring in his crops for him. His arrogance is greater than his honor."

Bassadjalan said, "Numuke, you must perform a service for me. I want you to carry a message to the terrace of heroes." In the late afternoon when the heroes were gathered at the terrace, the numuke went to that place, and Didiya Tiekele spoke condescendingly, saying, "Aaah, blacksmith, you come to drink with the noble heroes?" The blacksmith answered, "No, Master, I am not a noble but only a numuke. Bassadjalan Zambele asked me to come with a message. As everyone knows, when he arrived here he was a young man who had no fault to find with anyone. But the heroes derided him and made his life difficult. Then they enticed him to join them in a fight against Zanke and the town of Koble, but they abandoned him and left him to fight alone. Bassadjalan wants me to say that the six brothers have lost their honor, but because of their two sisters he will not punish them. Bassadjalan says that you, Didiya Tiekele, are the greatest hero in Kala. Therefore it is you he challenges. He says, 'You, Tiekele of Didiya, meet me in battle tomorrow morning and prove your valor.'" When Didiya Tiekele heard this he was elated. He said, "Ééé! This boy named Bassadjalan, his life is over!"

It happened that the morning set for the fight was the day all the townspeople were supposed to go out and harvest Didiya Tiekele's crops for him. So Didiya Tiekele ordered the people to gather on the walls and rooftops instead to observe the battle. He said, "When the fight is over and Bassadjalan is dead I will give away all his cattle. I will give his cows to the nobles, the leatherworkers, the ironworkers, the women and the children of Kala. Just as he arrived here without a name, he will depart without a name. The hyenas and eagles will eat his remains and there will be nothing left to remind the world that he ever lived."

There were men in Kala who went to counsel him. They quoted a proverb: "If you see a beautiful calabash floating down the river, do not be quick to claim it, for it may not be good. If it has floated past village after village and no one had taken it, there must be a good reason." They said to Didiya Tiekele, "Do not be quick to claim Bassadjalan Zambele. He has accomplished heroic deeds. It is clear that he has a powerful force within him." The warning only angered Didiya Tiekele. He answered, "Do not speak to me in this manner. My grandfather was great, my father was great, and I surpass everyone in my family who came before me. Who has ever defeated me in battle?"

In the morning when the sky became light, the two men rode to meet each other outside the town walls. The four gates were bolted from inside so that neither man, sensing defeat, could seek sanctuary within Kala. The townspeople stood on the walls and the rooftops to see the combat. Didiya Tiekele pointed his gun and fired, but the powder merely fizzled and the bullet fell harmlessly from the barrel. He rode away and started again, but once more his bullet would not fly. Three times he did this, and the third time it was the same. Then Bassadjalan came riding toward Didiya Tiekele as if to shoot, but instead he struck Didiya Tiekele with the magic garan given to him by his father. When Didiya Tiekele felt the blow he fell from his horse, crying out in pain. Bassadjalan dismounted and beat Didiya Tiekele with the garan. He struck again and again, Didiya Tiekele crying out over and over, "Ou-iii! Ou-iii!"

Inside the town the people could hear the crying, and they wondered that such a sound should come from a battle between two heroes. Soon they saw the two men coming toward the walls, Bassadjalan striking with his garan and Didiya crying out in terror and pain. When they reached the gate, Bassadjalan motioned as if to kill Didiya Tiekele, but the people interceded, saying, "There is no need to kill him, Bassadjalan. He is crying like a child. He is finished. He was a noble once, he was a hero once, he was a champion once, but he is nothing now and no one in Kala can take him seriously anymore." It was true. All the men and women who once harvested Didiya Tiekele's fields because they feared him now laughed and went back to their own work.

Bassadjalan did not kill Didiya Tiekele. He said, "No, I will not kill him, because he is afraid. It is not honorable to kill a man who is afraid. Yesterday he said he was the greatest of heroes. No man can properly say such a thing. He can say, 'I am the greatest of my mother's sons.' But he cannot say, 'I am the greatest of all mothers' sons.' A man may be strong and have many victories, but he must never forget that some day a hero with a smaller name may come and bring the glory to an end. Because he was not generous and just with other people, Didiya Tiekele's fate will be worse than death. In time, people will no longer remember him as a noble."

Bassadjalan took his cattle and his army of hunters and went back to the village of his parents. He was welcomed there as a person who had gone away to prove his valor and returned as an achiever of great deeds. He lived on, and in later years he went to another place and founded a city and a kingdom of his own. He lived, he died. But Bassadjalan was not forgotten, and in the words of the bards, his name was written in golden ink in the story of Segu.

SOKUFO SERIBA, A DJELI OF SEGU

THIS IS THE STORY OF SOKUFO SERIBA, a djeli who lived in the time of King Da Djera of the family of Traore. Da Djera had several djeli at his court, and all of them were master musicians. Their knowledge of the Traore family was extensive, and all were renowned for their playing of the ngoni. Sokufo Seriba was a favorite with Da Djera above the others, for his people had provided djeli for the king's family for many generations, and his praise songs were exceedingly beautiful. He lived outside Segu City in a large village called Jala Bugu, and whenever the king needed him he came with his ngoni, riding on a fine horse which Da Djera had given him. Da Djera lavished many gifts on Sokufo Seriba. He gave him gold, cowries, land, cattle and slaves. Because of the king's generosity, Sokufo Seriba was a rich man. He had three wives, a good house and everything a person could wish for in this world.

Now, though a king's djeli was a man of prestige, and though he might be a king's personal adviser, he was a person of caste and not noble. He learned his art from his father, who was not noble, and his father learned from his own father, who was not noble. Even though a djeli could be an interpreter and spokesman for the king, even though his name was known to people in distant cities, still he could not call himself noble. For a numuke, a blacksmith, was born to be a numuke; a leatherworker, no matter how famous, was born to be a leatherworker; a djeli, no matter how much he pleased a king, was a born djeli; and a noble, whether rich or poor, was a born noble.

Sokufo Seriba saw that he was more prestigious than many nobles in Segu. He became very proud. He thought, "I have everything. I have slaves, I have land, I have more cowries and gold than I can spend, and my cattle are beyond counting. So in what way am I less than noble?" He decided to live as a great man in his village and be a djeli no longer. Da Djera did not oppose Sokufo Seriba in what he wanted to do. He said, "If a ngoni does not wish to give out music, who can force it to do so?"

So Sokufo Seriba gave up coming to Segu City and lived in Jala Bugu. Whereas formerly the people there had always called him Djeli Sokufo Seriba, or sometimes Djeliba, meaning great djeli, now he insisted that he be called Baba Seriba, that is, Father Seriba. And to end the memory that he was born a djeli, he destroyed the ngoni on which he had played for the king and other notables of Segu. Though he never said aloud, "I am noble," still he behaved as if he were noble.

Then, in time, unfortunate things began to happen to Sokufo Seriba. First his cattle became ill and began to die. His herds diminished, and a day came when they were totally gone. The same thing happened to his sheep, his goats and his poultry. His fields did not yield millet as they should. He spent his money. His cowries and gold began to disappear. As if this were not enough, a day came when Sokufo Seriba's eyes became afflicted and he lost his sight. If a doctor came to the village, people would say, "Go and do something for Sokufo Seriba. He used to be the king's djeli, but now he is poor and blind." But the doctors could not cure Sokufo Seriba's blindness. His slaves left him because he could not take care of them. People gave him food from their own granaries. Sokufo Seriba was helpless. And when it seemed that he could not fall any lower, he lost his favorite wife. A handsome numuke of the village persuaded her to leave Sokufo Seriba, telling her, "Your husband has thrown away his life. He was once a great djeli and the king honored him. But he was not satisfied. He wanted more of everything. Now he is nothing. He has found poverty. He gropes in the darkness. His money is gone and his slaves are gone. His house disintegrates. You are a beautiful woman. If you come and live with me, I will make your life good." At last Sokufo Seriba's wife abandoned him and became the wife of the numuke. Of all the things Sokufo Seriba had valued, only his young son remained.

He lived in this condition of misery a long while. Then one morning he called his son and said, "Take me into the bush. Let us search and find a dead horse." The boy held the end of Sokufo Seriba's staff and led him into the bush. They searched, and after a while the boy said, "Father, here is a dead horse." Sokufo Seriba said, "Place my hand on its tail." The boy did so, and his father took his knife from his scabbard and cut the hairs from the tail. They returned home, and Sokufo Seriba laid the horsehairs on a mat and sorted them out with his fingers. On that day he began to make a new ngoni with horsehair strings. Even without sight, Sokufo Seriba could carve the form of the ngoni perfectly, for the ngoni was like an extension of his own body.

A day came when his ngoni was finished. He picked up the instrument and played it. The sound that the ngoni made was new. The manner in which Sokufo Seriba played was new. Its rhythm was new, and he sang in a way that had never before been heard in Segu. His words were:

> Da Djera, the cowries are gone.
> Da Djera, the gold is gone.
> When the money is gone I must go to Segu
> To see Da Djera who is the king of money.
> Da Djera, the slaves are gone.
> Da Djera, the fields are barren.
> When everything is gone I must go to Segu
> To see Da Djera who owns everything.

61

He put down his ngoni, saying to his son, "Tomorrow I shall go to Segu."

The next morning he hung his ngoni on his shoulder, took up his staff and said to his son, "Very well, now let us go to the house of Da Djera." The son took one end of the staff and led Sokufo Seriba to the gate of the king's compound in Segu. The king's guards stopped them at the gate and asked what they wanted. Sokufo Seriba said, "I am a djeli, as you can see. I have a song for the king." The guards reported to the king's counselors, saying, "There is a disreputable-looking person at the gate. His clothes are in tatters. He is blind. He says, 'I have a song for Da Djera.'" The counselors went to the gate. They asked, "Why do you want to see the king?" He answered, "I am a djeli. I have a song for the king. He would not want you to refuse me." Da Djera heard the conversation from inside, and he ordered Sokufo Seriba to be admitted. They brought him in. So much had Sokufo Seriba changed because of his misfortunes that the counselors did not recognize him. Only the king perceived who he was.

Sokufo Seriba sat down before Da Djera. Without any explanation he took his ngoni in his hands and played it in a way that had never before been heard in Segu. It was a new style of djuru unlike the old wolosekoro. It had a new sound that astonished the court. Sokufo Seriba sang:

> I lived in sickness and poverty.
> I thought, "I will go to Segu
> Where Da Djera, the lion, has his house.
> I will ask Da Djera to forgive me."
>
> Now I am in Segu in the presence of Da Djera.
> Across the river the poor people of Bakofela
> Cannot taste the wine of Segu.
> How unfortunate they are.
>
> A man who does not have a child of his own is poor.
> He can only watch the children of others playing.
> A king who does not have his own true djeli is poor.
> He can only listen to the djeli of other families.
>
> In Segu, Da Djera has all things.
> He is the owner of the water,

He is the owner of the wine,
He is the owner of the slaves,
He is the owner of the cowries,
He is the owner of the gold.

A father can have a good character,
Yet his son can take the wrong road.
A king can have a good character,
Yet his djeli can take the wrong road.
But whatever happens,
A man's son is his son forever.
Whatever happens,
A king's djeli is his djeli forever.

Da Djera, lion of the bush,
King of the Bambara,
Ruler over Maraka cities,
Ruler over Manding cities,
Ruler over Foulani cities,
You did everything for me
And I ask you to forgive me.

When Da Djera heard this song he was delighted. Sokufo Seriba's words touched him, and he thought, "I never had a djeli to surpass him. I should have kept him here and cared for him." And the king was entranced by the new style of djuru. He asked his other two djeli if they could play this way, and they did so, adapting Sokufo Seriba's words:

Let us go to Da Djera,
Let us go to the father of Segu.
If we have no cowries,
We go to Da Djera.
If we have no gold,
We go to Da Djera.
Da Djera has everything.

Thus Sokufo Seriba brought a new form of djuru to the king's court, and Da Djera was so pleased that he forgave him for going away and trying to live like a noble.

63

Da Djera restored his old djeli to honor. He ordered food and wine brought to Sokufo Seriba and gave him gifts. Then he sent an emissary to the village of Jala Bugu with this decree: "Da Djera, king of Segu, gives this village to Djeliba Sokufo Seriba. Henceforth Sokufo Seriba will handle all affairs of state and collect taxes for the king. Whatever he asks you to do, do it for him. Speak to him with respect. What Sokufo Seriba wants, the king wants."

When Sokufo Seriba returned to Jala Bugu the people received him with honor, for they had no choice but to do what Da Djera had ordered. Sokufo Seriba was now their "small king." Although they had no desire to be ruled by a man who was not from a noble line and who was blind, no one dared voice such a thought. In every respect Jala Bugu became Sokufo Seriba's village. Da Djera sent him gold, cattle and slaves to work his fields.

The first thing that Sokufo Seriba did was to order the people of Jala Bugu to come and make bricks and build a wall around his grounds. He said, "The wall must be completed in two days." Everyone in the village except workers in special crafts came and commenced the task. They dug earth, mixed it with water and animal hair, and made bricks that they set in the sun to dry. They made the wall in two days. Sokufo Seriba said, "Now make more bricks and build my house in the style of Da Djera's house." They tore down the ruins of his old house and began the construction.

While the construction was going on, Sokufo Seriba said, "I want seven of the strongest men in the village to come here." The people selected seven strong men and brought them, saying, "Baba Sokufo Seriba, here are the men." Sokufo Seriba said, "Stop calling me Baba. I am a djeli. I want to be called a djeli." They answered, "Yes, Djeli Sokufo Seriba." He said to the seven strong men, "Go out into the bush and cut as many tree branches as you can carry. Trim them and bring them to me. I want switches to beat the numuke who stole my favorite wife." They went out, they returned with many switches.

After that Sokufo Seriba called the slave boy of the numuke. He said, "My son, you were here when this tree was planted. You were here when this tree grew. You will be here when this tree gives fruit. Do you agree?" The boy said, "Yes," for he understood what the djeli was saying. The meaning was, "You were here when I was made chief. You were here when I announced I would punish the numuke. You will be here when the numuke is beaten." Sokufo Seriba then said, "My son, go and speak to your master with intelligence."

The boy understood what Sokufo Seriba meant by "intelligence." At the far end of the village he saw his master coming in from the bush on a horse. The numuke said, "Aaah! At last you become visible. Where have you been instead of at the forge? The iron is not red. Get to the bellows at once." The boy said, "Yes, Master, I will do it. I was in the town with the others because I was called to work on the construction." The numuke replied, "What construction is that?" for he had been away and knew nothing of what was happening. The boy said, "The wall and the new house that Sokufo Seriba has ordered us to build." The numuke exclaimed, "Aaah! Sokufo Seriba?" The boy said, "Yes, Da Djera has appointed him chief of the village. Da Djera has given him everything in Jala Bugu." The numuke said, "Everything?" They boy said, "Yes, Sokufo Seriba is the chief of everything. He selected seven men and sent them into the bush for whips." The numuke said, "Aaah!" The boy went on, "Yes, I heard him say he is going to punish the person who stole his wife." The numuke said, "Aaah!" He turned his horse back toward the bush, saying to the boy, "Get back to the forge. I will come later." And he rode away swiftly into the bush to find a place to hide.

The boy then returned to Sokufo Seriba and said, "I went there, but he is not at his forge." Sokufo Seriba ordered the people to search the village house by house, and they did so, but they did not find the numuke. Sokufo Seriba said, "Very well. Now search the bush." So the men formed small groups and went searching outside the village, calling, "Numuke! Numuke!" Because he had not had time to bring food and water, the numuke was not far away and was easy to find. Whenever a group of men came to his hiding place they said to him, "Ééé! What are you doing here? Why aren't you running? If you are caught, Sokufo Seriba will have you beaten until all the whips are broken. That is what he said." So the numuke would run from that place and find another place to hide. When another group found him they told him the same thing. Again the numuke ran. This went on all day, and when darkness fell, the men returned and said to Sokufo Seriba, "We searched everywhere in the bush, but as you can see, we did not find him."

Sokufo Seriba said, "Very well. Now go to the numuke's house and bring me my wife." They did this. The djeli announced that whenever the numuke was seen he should be apprehended. But people of the village did not want to see the numuke punished. In the darkness of night they went secretly to his hiding place and brought him home so that he could gather his belongings. He took everything that he, his family and his slaves could carry and departed from Jala Bugu. He abandoned the village forever, and finally settled in a remote part of the kingdom of Segu.

As for Sokufo Seriba, he governed Jala Bugu with good will and restraint, remembering that he was a djeli and not a noble. He administered the village for seven years, and went to Segu City only to sing for Da Djera on great occasions. At the end of the seven years he said to Da Djera, "You made me a 'small king' in Jala Bugu. I am grateful for what you did for me. But my heart is not in ruling a village. My heart is in my ngoni, in creating praise songs recalling the accomplishments of the Traore family. This is enough for me, so I give Jala Bugu back to you." He sang to Da Djera:

> *A hero is born to be a hero.*
> *A numuke is born to be a numuke.*
> *A djeli is born to be a djeli.*
> *If I am poor, still I am a djeli.*
> *If I am rich, still I am a djeli.*
> *If my eyes see, still I am a djeli.*
> *If I am blind, still I am a djeli.*
> *In my heart is the spirit of a djeli.*
> *It puts poetry in my mouth*
> *And my mouth sings poetry.*
> *It puts music in my fingers*
> *And my fingers play my ngoni.*
> *When I was poor I said,*
> *"This is not the meaning of my life."*
> *When I ruled Jala Bugu I said,*
> *"This is not the meaning of my life."*

SOKUFO SERIBA, A DJELI OF SEGU

The meaning of my life
Is that I will sing for the Traore family of kings.

Da Djera said, "Sokufo Seriba, you are my own true djeli. You made a sad mistake, but you have retrieved it."

Da Djera and Da Monzon Against Samaniana Bassi

WHEN DA DJERA RULED THE KINGDOM of Segu it became very powerful. The songs of the djeli tell us that Da Djera's boatmen patrolled the River Joliba and controlled its commerce, and that his Tonjon consisted of two hundred sixty battalions in the region of the capital and sixty battalions in outlying regions. Although Segu was a Bambara kingdom, when it expanded to north, east, south and west it became master of many towns and cities belonging to the Fula, the Manding and the Maraka, otherwise known as Soninke.

There was a large Fula city called Samaniana which had never become a vassal to Segu. Its king was Bassi, of the Djakite family, and he was known as Samaniana Bassi. The Fula were slightly built, and they were deemed by the Bambara to be inferior at war, yet when they were tested in battle they proved themselves to be fierce and courageous fighters unwilling to accept defeat. Samaniani Bassi and his people were Muslims, and for this reason they looked down on the Bambara as unbelieving pagans.

It is not said whether Da Djera did it to provoke the Fula ruler, but one day he sent his chief djeli to Samaniana with a message for Bassi. The message was that Da Djera would like to have Bassi's daughter for his wife. Bassi accepted the message as a great insult. He said to the djeli, "Tell Da Djera for me that he is not a hero. He is a common man who does not come from a noble line. Indeed, he is a slave in masquerade. He is not a believer in Allah. He is uncivilized and, moreover, he is an ugly man. Tell him never to speak again of marrying my daughter."

When the djeli returned, he delivered the message from Bassi word for word. Da Djera became angry. He said, "I want Samaniana." That is to say, he wanted the destruction of Bassi and his kingdom. He called an assembly of his counselors and asked for their advice on how the conquest should be carried out. They advised Da Djera not to undertake an expedition against Samaniana without great preparation. They said, "Your soldiers can fight valiantly, but without the power of medicine they cannot win." So Da Djera sent for his morikes and his filelikelas, his practitioners of mystic sciences, and asked them to devise protection for his fighters. The morikes and filelikelas divined with kolas and sand. And when they had read the meanings of their divinations, they returned to the king and said, "Great Da Djera, do not think that victory over Samaniana Bassi will come easily. It will be battle after battle, and many men will die. The divinations say that one day Samaniana will fall to you, but they do not say when this will happen. We can give protective magic to your fighters, but Bassi's fighters also will have protective magic. We can make your spears and bullets fly straight, but Bassi's morikes can do the same for him. Bullets and spears will meet each other in the air. It will require battle after battle to conquer Samaniana, perhaps war after war."

Da Djera heard their words. But he was eager to subdue Samaniana Bassi. He ordered the two hundred sixty Tonjon battalions in Segu City to assemble, and he sent for the sixty Tonjon battalions from outlying regions. He ordered the masiba dunu, the great war drum, to be played. The players of the war drum were lepers and albinos. Within two days Da Djera's army was ready. They were told that the next morning they would go on an expedition against Samaniana Bassi. So the fighting men of Segu feasted, drank wine, danced and boasted. Every hero declared his bravery and promised what he would do in battle, saying such things as, "When I get to Samaniana I will kill the king, I will do this, I will do that." They described vividly the feats they were going to perform. The following day they took the road to Samaniana.

When they arrived at the walls of Samaniana, Da Djera sent an emissary to Bassi with these words: "Da Djera of Segu sends his respect to King Bassi. The notables of Segu send their respect, the women of Segu send their respect, and the court counselors send their respect. So, also, do the officers of the Tonjon, the morikes, the blacksmiths and the slaves of Segu." Bassi Samaniana replied: "Tell Da Djera that we reciprocate his greetings. Tell him he and his Tonjon are welcome. It is growing dark now, it is too late for him to begin what he came to do. Therefore we open our gates so that he and his people can come in and share our food and wine."

Segu's fighters left their weapons in their camp and entered the city, where they ate and were entertained. There was drumming and dancing, and wine was plentiful. When the first hint of daylight came, Da Djera's fighters returned to their camp outside the walls, took up their weapons and prepared to fight. The warriors of King Bassi emerged from the city. There were battle cries from both armies and the fighting began. The struggle was hard. When Segu's warriors came forward, they were driven back. Da Djera's men would rest, then come forward again. Again they were driven back. When nightfall came, Segu's fighters retired to their camp and Samaniana's fighters went inside the city walls. The battle resumed the next morning at daybreak. It surged back and forth, and many men died, but there was no resolution. They fought a third day and a fourth, but Bassi's forces were resolute. The fighting went on so long it seemed that war was the natural order of things, like the rising and setting of the sun. At last Da Djera took his army back to Segu to rest and prepare for another expedition.

But at this time Da Djera fell sick. And when he saw how things were with him, he sent word to his twenty-two sons asking them to come and meet with him. When they were all assembled he said to them, "My sons, my light is dimming. We will talk further of it, but for now I have something for you to do. Each of you must go out and bring a short stick to me." The sons went out and returned, each with a short stick. Da Djera said, "Good. Break your sticks in half." They did so, and Da Djera took the forty-four half sticks and tied them tightly into a bundle. He said, "Each of you could break a single stick, but can anyone break this bundle?" They tried, and no one could break it.

Da Djera said, "I am going to explain to you the meaning of what we have done. One stick can be broken easily. This is what will happen if you each go your own way alone. Your enemy will break you. But if you stay bound together the enemy can never break you. I want you to pledge now, as we sit together, that you will never separate from one another, that you will always be united so that Segu will continue to live." The sons promised Da Djera that it would be this way. He placed the bundle of sticks in a calabash, which he hung over the doorway. He said, "Whenever you enter this room or depart from it you will see the calabash. Knowing what is in it, you will be reminded of your pledge."

When the sons left the meeting, Da Djera asked his eldest son, Da Monzon, to remain behind. He said to him, "The ball of life is unwinding for me. I am reaching the end of my time. I want you to promise something. Whether I am alive or dead, I must have Samaniana Bassi's head. I expect you to become king of Segu when I die. There are other cities to be conquered, but Samaniana is big in my mind, for Bassi gave a provocation that cannot be forgiven." Da Monzon said, "My father, you can die in peace. Bassi's head will be brought to Segu and sacrificed to the Twelve Fetishes." Da Djera said, "That is good." Soon after that, Da Djera traveled to another city in Segu, where he died. The death ceremonies were conducted for ninety days.

Da Monzon went to his mother to speak to her about the kingship. He said, "I am Da Djera's eldest son. My father expected me to accept the responsibility. The ceremony should be held." But his mother, named Badjoni, restrained him, saying, "No, my son, it cannot be done that way. Call your brothers together. Tell them your father already did many things for you, and you are satisfied. Say that you are not looking to become king. In that way you will learn what is in their minds." Da Monzon followed Badjoni's advice. The brothers came together and discussed the kingship. Da Monzon said, "Now it must be decided. Segu is a body without a head. Although I am the eldest, I do not claim the kingship. I already have everything I need. Decide among yourselves what would be best. Let us remember the calabash of broken sticks. Whoever takes the responsibility will have the loyalty and support of all." His brothers answered, "No, eldest brother, it is right for you to become the king. Segu belongs to you. We belong to you. Our spears and guns belong to you. What you tell us to do, we will do. What you tell us not to do, we will not do. That is the only way it can be. If one of us were to become king, another might say, 'Why is he the one?' There would be dissension. You are the eldest. No one can dispute that you are the senior to all of us. Therefore it is you who will become king."

In this way Da Monzon became the ruler of Segu. And it came to be said of his mother, Badjoni, that she was the daughter, wife and mother of kings. For her father was a king; her husband, Da Djera, was a king; and her son, Da Monzon, was a king.

Da Monzon had many responsibilities, but in time he began to think about the war against Samaniana Bassi. He spoke to his counselors about it, and they reminded him of the failure of Da Djera's expedition. They said, "Great king of Segu, war is more than valor against valor, hero against hero, and will against will. There is also the question of who has superior medicine. Our filelikelas and morikes are masters of the mystic sciences. Samaniana Bassi also has masters of the mystic sciences. In the battles waged by your father against Bassi, force countered force, and the two forces neutralized each other. This time your doctors of the mystic forces must prepare you with a medicine beyond anything we have known in the past." Da Monzon's counselors gave him the names of the greatest morikes of Segu, and he sent for them to come to the palace.

The morikes came, and Da Monzon told them what he wanted. They went to their private places and divined, and after they were finished they returned to Da Monzon and said, "We have consulted with the mystic forces about the thing you want to do. You can defeat Bassi, but not without difficult preparation. We can make the required magic if we have certain things to work with." Da Monzon said, "What are the things? I will give you whatever you want."

73

They answered, "The things we need are things you do not have. We must have certain objects of clothing belonging to Samaniana Bassi: shoes that he has worn, a belt that he has worn and a hat that he has worn. With these things we can do the work that will assure your victory. If we do not have them there is no hope of success."

Da Monzon thought, "How will I ever get these objects? If I had already conquered Samaniana Bassi I could merely take them. But I cannot succeed in the conquest until I have them in my hand." So he assembled his counselors again and gave them the riddle to answer. They pondered. They said, "Do we have a hero in Segu who could enter Bassi's city, obtain the required things and return? No, we have no such hero." One of the elders among the counselors said, "If a man cannot accomplish such a thing perhaps a woman can. Certain things are beyond the powers of men, but history teaches us that sometimes a woman can accomplish what a man cannot. Let us find a woman who will go to Samaniana to get the shoes, the belt and the hat."

So Da Monzon called for all the young women of Segu to come to his court, and he said to them, "My father, Da Djera, refused to die without hearing the promise that Bassi's head would be brought to Segu. I am ready to make the expedition. But for the spiritual preparations the morikes must have three things: a hat that has been worn by Bassi, shoes that have been worn by Bassi and a belt that has been worn by Bassi. It will be a heroic accomplishment that only a woman can achieve. Is there a woman in Segu willing to undertake this task? If so, let her speak. If she succeeds, I promise to make her life bountiful. She and her family will always be in my favor, and she will receive from me one hundred of everything—cattle, slaves, cowries and gold."

A young woman named Djero said she could do what the king wanted. She specified what she would need for the enterprise: first, a gourd containing the honey drink called guibara; second, a young girl-slave to accompany her; a canoe; and twelve strong fishermen to man the canoe. The king ordered these things to be given to her. She went to her house and prepared. She asked a morike to place a charm on the honey drink to protect her, and he did so.

Djero was considered to be a very beautiful woman. The djeli of

Segu said that if a woman was beautiful, three parts of her body were generous and three parts were fine. A beautiful woman had generous hips, generous breasts and generous eyes. Her head was small and finely shaped, her neck was thin and long, and her waist was narrow. Poets had a saying that a beautiful woman had a skin so smooth that her waist was equal to a hundred-year trip of a louse. That was to say that a louse trying to travel around her waist would not be able to cling to her smooth skin and would constantly fall off, and it would take a hundred years to make the journey. Djero knew that because of her beautiful body and the magical lotion she had applied to it she would be able to accomplish her work.

Early in the morning she went to the canoe with her girl slave. The paddlers were waiting. Samaniana, like Segu, was on the River Joliba. The paddlers took Djero to a beach near the city, then hid themselves and their canoe in a bed of thick water grass and rushes. Djero removed her clothing and stood in the shallow water to bathe, while her slave girl waited on the bank. In time a man from Samaniana came by, and when he saw her he stopped to admire her beauty. He saw her narrow waist, her generous hips and breasts and her fine skin. He greeted her, saying, "Woman, are you human or a divine spirit?" She replied, "I am human." He asked, "Where are you coming from, and what are you doing here?" She replied, "I am coming from Kaarta, where my life is too hard, and I am going to the house of Da Monzon in Segu." The man left hurriedly and went to King Bassi, wanting to be the first to report what he had seen. He said, "Great king, if you do not obtain this woman for your wife you will be only half a king. She is beautiful beyond description."

Samaniana mounted his horse at once and rode to the place where Djero was bathing. He greeted her in the customary way, asking, "How are you? How is your father? How is your family? How is your village?" But Djero responded diffidently to his greetings, as if to say that the king did not impress her. When Bassi said, "Good morning," she answered, "Yes, it is morning, but I do not yet know whether it is good or not." When he asked, "How is your father?" she answered, "When your father dies you will know how good it is to have a father." Bassi asked, "How is your mother?" In the Bambara language the word for mother is *ba,* and the word for river also is *ba*. Djero played with the words, saying, "When you arrive at the ba and do not have a canoe to take you across, you will understand the importance of having a ba." The king asked, "How are your brothers?" In Bambara the word for brother is *kawraw*, and the word for old also is *kawraw*. Djero played with the words. She said, "When you become kawraw and discover that you do not have any kawraw to take care of you, you will understand that old age is something to fear." Bassi was delighted not only with her beauty but her agile use of language. He understood her to say that she had no parents and that she was looking for a better life for herself. He asked her where she was coming from and where she was going, and she answered, "I am coming from Kaarta and I am going to offer myself to Da Monzon in Segu."

Samaniana Bassi said, "Ééé, woman, you are wasting your time. Why would you go to Segu? Did you never hear my name? I am called Bassi." Djero answered, "Yes, I have heard the word *bassi*. It is the food prepared from millet flour." Djero's seeming disinterest in Bassi only heightened his desire for her. He said, "It would be foolish to go to Segu. Da Monzon is not a noble, but a slave. He is not a Believer, but a pagan. He is an ugly and dirty man. Do not throw yourself away. Stay here in Samaniana. Here you can be my wife and have all the good things you want in life."

Djero answered slowly, as if she were considering Bassi's arguments. She said, "Aaah, you go too fast. We have only just met. I do not know you, only that you call yourself by the same name as our most commonplace food in Kaarta. You, also, you do not know me. If I become one of your wives I will be bound just as if I were a slave. Let us go at it another way. I will agree to be your consort for a time. We will see how it goes. Later, if you want me as a wife you can send a messenger to my town and get permission from my family." Bassi said, "Yes, yes, that is the way we will do it." He instructed his slaves to take Djero's things and carry them. When she had put on her clothes, Bassi conducted her and the slave girl to the city. He gave her a house in his compound, but she herself was placed in Bassi's private sleeping quarters. The wives of the king lived in their separate houses, but Djero shared the king's house with him. Djero gave Bassi the gourd of charmed guibara. He drank it all, saying that none of his wives could make guibara as good as this.

Samaniana Bassi was so infatuated with Djero that he forgot he had wives. He slept with Djero every night. During the day she cooked for him and kept his house in order. Every afternoon she sent her slave girl to the river to wash the gourds and calabashes from which they ate. And as she became familiar with Bassi's house she found old clothing that he no longer wore. One by one she secured the objects she had come for: the shoes, the belt and the hat. On a certain day she put these objects in the large basket in which her slave girl carried the gourds and calabashes to the river. As she had been instructed, the girl took the objects to the paddlers where they were hiding with their canoe among the rushes.

Djero herself stayed with Samaniana Bassi, giving him wine to drink, first one gourdful then another. In time, Bassi's eyes began to droop and then he fell into a heavy sleep. Djero went out, telling anyone who saw her leave that she was going to the river to punish her slave girl for taking so long with her work. When Djero arrived at the river her slave girl and her paddlers were waiting for her. She entered the canoe and they began the return journey to Segu.

Samaniana Bassi slept for a long time. When he awoke he asked for Djero, and people told him she had gone to the river to punish her slave. Bassi sent a messenger to the river to ask Djero to return. The messenger came back, saying to the king, "The woman is not there. Her slave is not there. All that is there is the basket containing the dirty gourds and calabashes." The king began to realize his mistake. He understood now that Djero was not from Kaarta, but that she had been sent by Da Monzon. He ordered his own canoemen to pursue her, but they were too late.

When Djero arrived in Segu City she went to the king's house and delivered the objects she had stolen from Bassi. Da Monzon called his morikes and gave the objects to them. They began at once to do their work. They did various things known only to practitioners of the mystic sciences. After that they made a bundle containing King Bassi's belt, shoes and hat, and they tied the bundle to a very large rock. The rock was so heavy that it required seven men to lift it. The morikes said to Da Monzon, "We have done our work. If we have done it well, praise us. If we have done it badly, punish us. It is up to you to judge. As you see, the bundle containing Bassi's hat, belt and shoes is fastened to this rock. If what we have done is good, the

77

rock will float. If what we have done is worthless, the rock will sink. Have your men place it in the water." Seven of Da Monzon's strongest slaves carried the rock to the river, a large crowd following them. The rock was placed in the water. It did not sink. It floated as if it were a leaf, telling Da Monzon that he could now wage a successful war against Samaniana Bassi.

Da Monzon was happy. He rewarded his morikes for their work, giving them much gold and many cowries. He sent for Djero, and when she came he said to her, "Woman, you have done an exceptional deed. We have many strong men and many heroes in Segu, but none of them could possibly do what you have achieved. You have courage equal to that of any man. For what you have done I will give honors to you and your family, and I will also give you one hundred of everything—cattle, sheep, slaves and cowries. Segu will not forget you, and the djeli of future generations will praise you."

Da Monzon's army prepared for the war to come. They repaired their guns, made bullets and powder, sharpened their spears and knives, and had charms sewed into their clothing. The blacksmiths forged new weapons and the leatherworkers made shields for men and protective trappings for the horses. The preparations required six months, and then Da Monzon was ready. He led his army to the walls of Samaniana.

As his father had done before him, he sent an emissary with greetings for King Bassi. He said, "Valorous king of Samaniana, Segu sends respectful greetings. The nobles of Segu greet you, the women of Segu greet you, the djeli and people of caste greet you, the slaves of Segu greet you." And Bassi replied, "Welcome, my son, to Samaniana. May you and your army earn honor in what is to come. But before you act, think again. Your father could not win over us and he had to return empty-handed to Segu. What your great father could not do, you cannot do. You are wasting your time. Your dead will litter the earth and you, also, will have to leave with nothing to remember except defeat." Da Monzon answered, saying, "Great Bassi, the earth is made for heroes to stand on or lie upon. When was it ever different? Do not be misled because I am only a son of my father. There is a small vine in the bush that looks small and weak, but it can be woven into an unbreakable rope. I have promised my father that I will bring your head back to Segu, and that is why I am here."

After that, Samaniana threw open its gates to the visitors from Segu. Da Monzon's soldiers left their weapons in their camp and entered the city to feast, drink wine and dance. Only when the sky hinted at daylight did they leave and return to their camp. Da Monzon addressed the officers of the Tonjon. He said, "My officers, I came here for a victory and will not go back without it. Witness my words. I want the head of Samaniana Bassi. If we do not succeed, I will sacrifice you all to the Twelve Fetishes of Segu. It is Bassi's head or yours." When the war chiefs heard this they became solemn. They went back to their battalions and urged their men to fight valiantly.

As the dawn broke, Bassi's fighters came out of the city and the battle began. The struggle was bitter. As the djeli sometimes sang before a battle:

> To speak the word war
> Is sweeter than war itself.
> Many persons say "war" without knowing war.
> War makes many orphans.
> War turns wives into widows.
> War turns cities into ruins.
> War turns kings into slaves.
> War is not good.
> Yet without war there cannot be victory.

The fighting went on all day, and many men died. The fighting continued the second day, and the third, without either side gaining a victory. They fought seven days, and Samaniana Bassi's men still held fast.

Da Monzon's officers held a meeting to discuss ways of capturing the city. One of them suggested that the conquest might be accomplished with the complicity of Bassi's favorite wife, and they went to Da Monzon with this idea. He said, "Yes, very well, but how can it be done?" One of the officers of the Tonjon, named Korote Masigi, declared his confidence that he could gain access to the favorite wife through bribery if the king would provide him with the gold. The king provided the gold, and Korote Masigi found a way into the city and went to Bassi's royal compound. At the gate he bribed the guard with gold, and the guard let him pass. He still had to go through six bulos, or anterooms, in each of which a guard was stationed. He gave each of the guards gold and was allowed to pass through the six bulos. He was then in the royal courtyard, and he went to the house of the favorite wife.

He spoke with her softly. He made it known that he had come from Da Monzon, who wanted her to be his wife. She said, "I am the wife of Samaniana Bassi, the greatest of all men in the land of the Fula. Why should I want to be the wife of Da Monzon?" Korote Masigi said, "Da Monzon is the richest of men. He sends you this gift of gold as a small token. If you become his wife he will make you his favorite, and nothing will be too good for you." He described the splendors of Segu, and Da Monzon's generosity. He described Da Monzon himself, young and handsome. And at last the woman said, "I hear your words," meaning that she was willing. Korote Masigi said, "Da Monzon will be happy with what you are saying." She answered, "Whatever he wants, I will do it for him." Korote Masigi said, "Yes, he will make you prosperous and contented. He wants only that you moisten Bassi's gunpowder." And she said, "Tonight I will do it." Korote Masigi then left her and made his way back to Da Monzon's camp. He reported to the king that the shaft of Bassi's spear had been broken, meaning that the Fula king would be defenseless.

That night Bassi's favorite wife called her slave women to her house and ordered them to bring calabashes full of water. They brought the water, and she led them to the armory where the bullets and powder were stored. They poured water on the powder until it was sodden and useless, and afterward she sent a messenger to Korote Masigi to say that Bassi's spear had no shaft.

In the morning the army of Samaniana Bassi emerged from the city and the fighting was renewed. But when the sun was high in the sky their ammunition was running low, and they sent men to bring more bullets and powder. When the men arrived at the armory they found that the powder was spoiled. They went to Bassi and reported what they had learned. Bassi exclaimed, "Aaah!" He understood that he had been betrayed by his favorite wife, but he could not openly accuse her without evidence. He said, "Now I am finished, and Da Monzon will get my head." He sent messengers by secret routes to other Fula cities to ask for help, but he knew that time was against him because the distances were too great. He said to his favorite wife, "The light is fading for my city and my kingdom. There is nothing more that I can do. Still, I would like to deprive Da Monzon of my head. I will take my son and go down into my secret underground room. Perhaps they will not find me. You, my favorite wife, you alone will know where I am. When we have gone down, cover the opening and disguise it." Bassi and his son descended into the underground room, and his wife covered the opening with mats and skins.

Having no more gunpowder, Bassi's war chiefs came to ask him what to do, but they could not find him. They went to the house of his favorite wife and asked her if she had seen him. She said, "Yes, I will show you where he is." She took them to the underground hiding place and uncovered it, saying, "See, the king and his son are there." When the war chiefs saw Samaniana Bassi and his son down below, they laughed three times, "Ha ha ha!" in derision, for it was a dishonor for a king to behave in such a manner. Bassi came out. He also laughed three times, "Ha ha ha!" He said, "I did not go below with my son because of fear. I did it to discover without question who it was who betrayed the city. My wife knew she was not to reveal my whereabouts to anyone, but she eagerly told everyone where I was. It was she who wet the gunpowder and finished us." To his favorite wife he said, "Woman, you were the most favored wife among the Fula, but that day has ended. I will not kill you now, however, because your time is coming. Whatever Da Monzon promised you does not matter because we both will die."

The next day Da Monzon's army entered Samaniana, and Bassi, his son and his wife were taken as prisoners. The city was sacked and many people were taken as slaves. When the expedition returned to Segu, Da Monzon said to Bassi, "What my father wanted done I have accomplished. Because you are a noble you will speak fearlessly. My father sent an emissary to you to ask for your daughter. What I want to hear from your own mouth is the answer you gave him." Bassi replied, "Yes, I remember. I said he was not a hero. I said he was not a noble but a slave in masquerade. I said he was a Bambara unbeliever. I said he was uncivilized and ugly." Da Monzon said, "I thank you for what you have told me. Because you

81

speak with honor and without fear of the consequences, I can see that you are truly a noble. If I could spare your life I would do it. But I promised my father to take your head and sacrifice you to the Twelve Fetishes of Segu."

Samaniana Bassi said, "Yes, I know it. But I have a favor to ask." Da Monzon answered, "Yes, certainly. You are a hero and I cannot deny your request before you die." Bassi said, "The favor is this. My wife betrayed me and all my people. I would like to see her executed before my turn comes." Da Monzon asked the woman, "When you were living with Bassi what did he do for you?" She answered, "Aaah, I am a Fula, I will be truthful. Bassi was very kind to me. He made me his favorite wife. He raised me above all other Fula women. He made my family rich. I had many slaves. I never had to cook or do any washing." Da Monzon said, "If he did all of these things for you, what could you expect from me that would be better? You had everything. Still, you betrayed your husband. Why would you not do the same thing to me?" And he ordered the woman to be taken out and executed.

After that Da Monzon ordered Bassi to be killed. So his soldiers fired their guns at Bassi, but Bassi had great protective magic that had been given to him by his morikes, and the bullets would not penetrate his body. He said to Da Monzon, "Aaah! Do you expect to kill me with gunfire? No bullet can kill me, no spear can kill me, no metal can take my life." So Da Monzon called his morikes to divine for him how Bassi would be killed. They divined with kolas. They said to Da Monzon, "It is true. Bassi cannot be killed by metal. But the kolas tell us that wood can make him mortal." So a wooden knife was made, and with that knife Bassi was executed.

When this was done, Da Monzon sent for Korote Masigi, the man who had risked his life by going into Samaniana to corrupt Bassi's favorite wife. He said, "Korote Masigi, you are a valorous and artful man. You accomplished a great thing for me. If it had not been for you, we might still be standing outside the walls of Samaniana. You are a true hero of Segu. But I cannot let you live, for I would never be sure that you would not do a similar thing against me and thus cause the downfall of Segu." So Korote Masigi was led away and executed.

But Da Monzon did not execute Bassi's son or make him a slave, because he respected the bravery of his father. The boy lived on in Segu City and became a young man, and then he went away and established himself in another place. He never tried to avenge his father's death at Da Monzon's hands, and therefore he lost respect among the Fula people. The Fula declared that he was not noble but only half noble, and the same was said in later years about all his descendents. Even today a Fula noble will not give his daughter to anyone in this family.

Da Monzon's war against Samaniana was merely one of many conquests. He subjugated many cities, and under his rule Segu achieved its greatest power.

Da Monzon Against Chiaro Mamari

THE POETS SPEAK OFTEN in their songs about the Four Segus. That is their way of recalling the four original cities of the kingdom: Segu City, Chiaro, Mpeba and Welesedunu. In the days of Da Djera the four cities were like the fingers of a hand, and the thumb of the hand was the king. When Da Djera died and his son Da Monzon took power, the kingdom expanded greatly, and the four cities were likened to a constellation of stars. Around them and between them were lesser stars, smaller Bambara villages and also, here and there, villages of the Soninke, the Manding, the Fula and other peoples.

Da Monzon, when he became king, was not trustful of the other three cities because they were large and prosperous, and he was not certain of their loyalty. For this reason he sent secret agents to Chiaro, Mpeba and Welesedunu to mingle with the people and keep

85

track of what was happening. From time to time Da Monzon heard reports from Chiaro that disturbed his mind. No one could say with certainty that the chief, Chiaro Mamari, was disloyal in any way. But it was being said everywhere that life in Chiaro was just as good as in Segu City, and that Mamari was very popular with his people. There were even rumors that when the bards sang praise songs they spoke first of Mamari and only afterward of Da Monzon. Da Monzon thought, "This Mamari must be watched." Again he thought, "Mamari grows too important." And a time came when Da Monzon thought, "Mamari wants to take Chiaro away from Segu and have his own kingdom. He will have to be killed."

However, Mamari had never openly committed an act to merit such a punishment, so Da Monzon explored the problem with his counselors. They told him what he knew, that Chiaro Mamari could not be executed without an offense against the king. At last Da Monzon said, "Chiaro Mamari is a threat to Segu. If we wait until he gives us cause, it may be too late. Therefore let us contrive an offense." And so Da Monzon's counselors conspired to entrap Chiaro Mamari. The king sent a message to Chiaro Mamari asking him to come to Segu to participate in discussions about affairs of state. Mamari came to Segu. The king welcomed him. He gave him a house, slaves to care for his needs and women to cook his meals. Every morning Chiaro Mamari sat with other notable persons in the large chamber where the king heard pleas from citizens, settled disputes and discussed matters of importance.

One morning Da Monzon turned his head and spoke to some of his counselors in a low voice, but loud enough for Chiaro Mamari to overhear. What he said was that he was preparing a military expedition against a certain city in the kingdom. Now, the chief of that city was a cousin to Mamari, and Da Monzon anticipated that Mamari would warn his cousin and thereby commit an act of treason against the king. Mamari gave no sign that he had heard anything. He continued to attend the king's court. Then, after many days, he asked Da Monzon for permission to return to Chiaro. Da Monzon agreed, thanking Mamari for his visit and giving him slaves as a present.

Chiaro Mamari returned home, and he immediately sent a message to his cousin asking him to come on an urgent visit. When the two men were together they discussed many things, and then, when the moment was right, Mamari informed his cousin that Da Monzon was planning an expedition against him. But when he was communicating this information, no words passed through Mamari's lips. He kept his lips tightly closed and conveyed the information by gestures and signs. After that, the cousin returned to his own city and began preparations for its defense.

Da Monzon had no real intention of attacking the city. He wanted only to entrap Chiaro Mamari in a disloyal action. When his secret agents brought news that the city was preparing to defend itself, Da Monzon was assured that he now had cause to execute Mamari. Once more he invited Mamari to visit the capital, and Mamari came even though he remembered the saying: "When a person is called to Segu by the king, he can never be sure that he will return home." This time he was not given a house by the king, and so he stayed in the home of Ngoroni, a djeli of the court. While Mamari rested there, Ngoroni said to him, "Mamari, you yourself must know why you are here again. The last time you were in Segu the king spoke secretly to his counselors about plans to attack your cousin's city. Afterward you warned your cousin. Now Da Monzon will accuse you of treason." Chiaro Mamari answered, "Aaah, yes, I know that Da Monzon wants my head. But if I did not come I would lose honor. If I were a slave I would run. But I am a noble. Let him tell me to my face."

The next morning Chiaro Mamari attended the king's court. After other business had been disposed of, Mamari announced himself to the djeli, saying, "Da Monzon asked me to come, so I am here. I bring him good wishes from the people of Chiaro, the nobles, the people of caste and the slaves." The djeli repeated the greeting to the king. Da Monzon answered, "Chiaro Mamari, what you did was wrong. You committed a grave fault. The last time you were at my court you happened to overhear something I said in confidence to my counselors, that I was planning an attack against your cousin's city. You carried this information to your cousin, and now his city is preparing to defend itself. What you have done is a serious matter, for nothing is worse than treason to Segu. You understand the consequences of your actions."

Chiaro Mamari spoke quietly and respectfully to Da Monzon, saying, "Great king of Segu, if I ever said with my mouth any secret I heard in your court, let the Twelve Fetishes of Segu destroy me here and now. If I ever said with my mouth that you were planning to attack my cousin's city, let the Twelve Fetishes take me. What I am accused of telling never passed my lips." In the Bambara language, if one "says" something it is expressed as "says with the mouth." When Chiaro Mamari had warned his cousin, he had done so with pressed lips, indicating only by hand signs what was going to happen. Therefore when he told the king, "I never said with my mouth," he was speaking a literal truth. And when he swore to this before the Twelve Fetishes it was a great and powerful oath.

There was stillness in the court. Because of the great oath he had sworn, and because the Twelve Fetishes did not immediately destroy him, the assemblage was convinced of Mamari's truthfulness. Everyone waited for the king to speak. At last he said, "Aaah, Mamari! You are not guilty." And instantly the court djeli improvised a song:

> *Suspicion about a man is not enough.*
> *What is important is his guilt or innocence.*
> *People had bad thoughts about Chiaro Mamari,*
> *But we find that he is innocent.*

Mamari returned home to Chiaro knowing that Da Monzon had no intention of letting him live forever. So he quietly began to do what was necessary to defend Chiaro. He strengthened his army, repaired the walls of the city, and ordered his blacksmiths to make weapons. All of these things were reported to Da Monzon by his agents. Yet this was not enough for Da Monzon to act, for every city in the kingdom had its army, its walls and its weapons. But while doing what he was doing, Chairo Mamari neglected to send the annual price-of-the-honey to Da Monzon. Failure to send the annual taxes in combination with Mamari's preparation for defense gave Da Monzon what he needed. It was a signal that Chiaro was renouncing Segu as its master. Da Monzon sent a message to Mamari that said, "I see that you have aspirations for yourself. Therefore I am coming to visit you. There is not sufficient room on a riverbank for two male hippopotamuses to live together."

Chiaro Mamari's counselors pleaded with him not to accept the challenge from Da Monzon. They said, "Let us not fight. Tell Da

Monzon that Chiaro remains loyal to him. We will do whatever he wants." Mamari answered, "We are nobles. If we debase ourselves, what shall we tell our children tomorrow? There can be no honorable destiny without courage." To the messenger who had come from Segu, Mamari said, "Tell Da Monzon this: When his father, Da Djera, was alive we nobles in Chiaro supported him in every way. When he needed fighters we gave him fighters. When he needed gold we gave him gold. Every year we sent the taxes without exception. You also, Da Monzon, whatever you needed from us, we gave it. Only this year have we failed to send the-price-of-the-honey, but it did not have an inner meaning. We still plan to send you the taxes. I have never done anything to injure you. If you hold the-price-of-the-honey against me, then you will have to come to do what you think you have to do. I will prepare myself. Segu is welcome to come to Chiaro." In the way he phrased his message, Mamari implied that henceforth Chiaro would have its own identity and that it was prepared to fight to preserve itself.

Da Monzon organized his expedition. He sent for his practitioners of the mystic sciences, both his filelikelas, who were Bambara, and his morikes, who were Muslims. They divined to see the future, and each in his own way came to the same answer. They told Da Monzon, "You will win in the end because you have a great army of powerful fighters. Yet it will not be an easy victory. The people of Chiaro will fight valiantly, and you will not be able to win in less than forty-one days. You will destroy Chiaro, but the kolas say that you will never have Mamari's head."

In Chiaro, Mamari consulted his chief morike, Bani Traore, who told him, "Mamari, Da Monzon's forces are as numerous as grains of sand in the desert. Even if every man, woman, slave and child in Chiaro were a hero, still you could not win over Da Monzon's army. If you kill a thousand of the enemy, another thousand will appear, and yet another thousand, and another. Da Monzon will never turn back. Soften his feelings. Do not let the first blows be struck, because after that it will be too late, and pleading with Allah will be useless." Mamari would not bend. He said, "No, I will not demean myself with Da Monzon. All men die, and if I die tomorrow I will not die the day after."

Bani Traore said, "Mamari, look around you. Look at your city. It is peaceful. The people are working. You can hear the women pounding millet. You can hear the numukes shaping iron at their forges. You can hear children playing in the streets. Outside the walls the men are in their fields and cattle are grazing. Chiaro is alive, and people in faraway places speak of your city. But if Da Monzon comes with his armies many valiant heroes will die and free people will become slaves. Chiaro will return to the earth from which it came, and grass will grow over it."

Mamari listened to his morike, but nothing could change his mind. His favorite wife tried to influence him, but his mind was set. He sent messages to chiefs of other towns asking for help, but most of them were reticent, thinking, "Even if we all went to Mamari's aid, who could hold off Da Monzon?" Bani Traore tried one last time. He said, "Mamari, your army is big and full of heroes. A canoe can be large also, and have many men in it, but it can be swallowed by the river." Mamari said, "My friend, you mean well. But you cannot persuade me. I come from a noble line. My family helped build the kingdom of Segu. They built with respect, courage and honor. If it is my fate to die, this I can tell you: I will never become a slave, and my body will never be taken to Segu."

On a certain day, Da Monzon launched his expedition from Segu. He arrived at Chiaro and camped outside the walls. He sent a message to Mamari with respectful greetings, saying, "I bring you good wishes from the people of Segu, from the nobles, the djeli, the counselors of the court, the people of caste, the women and the slaves." Mamari answered, "Da Monzon, you are welcome here." But he also said, "Just at this moment I am in my house without shoes on my feet, clothes on my body or a hat on my head. Give me time to dress myself." By these words Chiaro Mamari was saying, "Excuse me. I am not yet quite ready to fight. Please wait a little." And Da Monzon responded, "Yes, if I come too early I am sorry. Take two more weeks."

During those two weeks Mamari continued to ask help from other cities. And though they had been reluctant before, they began to say, "If Chiaro is treated this way, we could be next." Some of the cities sent fighters to help Mamari, and many heroes hoping to prove their valor went of their own accord. In this way the fighting forces of Chiaro became stronger. When the two weeks had passed, Da

Monzon sent an envoy to Mamari to ask, "Do you have shoes on your feet, clothes on your body and a hat on your head?" Mamari answered, "Yes, I am clothed." And so, at last, the fighting began outside the walls of Chiaro.

Day after day the two armies fought, stopping only at nightfall. In the gray light of morning the armies clashed again. The dust and smoke of the battle rose into the sky and hung like a dark cloud. Many heroes on both sides fought their last fight, and some youths new to battle became heroes. Countless nobles of Chiaro and Segu embraced the earth, and many women of the two cities became widows. After fifteen days Da Monzon took his fighters back to Segu to rest and repair their weapons. Then they returned to Chiaro and the fighting resumed anew. Each day the two armies struggled from morning until night. Again Da Monzon took his fighters back to Segu to rest. The blacksmiths of the city made gunpowder and bullets, repaired guns, restored broken spear shafts, and through knowledge known only to them they gave magic powers to the weapons. Da Monzon's army went a third time to Chiaro. The battle was ruthless, and the battlefield claimed men of youth and men of old age. It seemed as if all the men of Segu and all the men of Chiaro would disappear from life and leave only women and children behind.

Da Monzon's morike said to him, "Do not forget the divination. You cannot win before forty-one days. Do not waste the men of Segu." So Da Monzon revised his strategy. He encircled Chiaro and put the city under siege, so that neither food nor reinforcements could enter. The city became hungry. Mamari's soldiers tried to break the siege, but they could not do it.

A day came when Chiaro Mamari knew the end was not far away. He sent for his favorite wife and his son to meet with him. He sent also for his chief djeli, his chief numuke, the chief of his slaves and his most trusted counselors. He said, "Everything is nearly over. I am going to die, but I don't want my head taken to Segu. When I am dead, bury me secretly in the earth beneath my personal room. Da Monzon must never know of it." Mamari ordered an old, faithful counselor to shoot him. The old man seemed not to be able to raise his gun. Mamari said, "We have known each other all our lives. Do what I ask as a friend. Otherwise I will order a slave to do it." So the old man raised his gun and killed Mamari. They carried his body into his room and buried it under the earthen floor. They brought dry earth and covered the grave with it, until there was no sign that the floor had been disturbed.

Mamari's favorite wife said, "They will take me to Segu as a slave. I cannot accept such a fate. Like Mamari, I prefer to die here." Mamari's chief djeli said, "I belong to Mamari. I am the keeper of his history and the composer of his praise songs. I refuse to be a slave djeli in Da Monzon's court. I will die here instead." Mamari's chief numuke said, "I am the one who made the king's spear and gun. I made the metal bit for his horse's mouth. I carved wood and made silver bowls for him. I made magical objects to protect him. I have done everything. I do not choose to go to Segu as a slave. Therefore I also will give myself the gift of death in Chiaro."

So Mamari's favorite wife, his chief djeli and his chief numuke went into the third bulo, or chamber, through which people had to pass to reach Mamari's personal quarters. The numuke spread gunpowder on the floor, and after that they waited. Meanwhile, Da Monzon's Tonjon was breaching the walls of the city, and when it had broken through, a party of thirty men rushed to the king's compound to make Mamari a prisoner. They entered the first bulo, which was empty, and then into the second bulo, which also was empty. When they reached the third bulo they found Mamari's favorite wife, his djeli and his numuke sitting there on skins. The soldiers shouted, "Where is Chiaro Mamari?" But they received no answer. And before they could pass into the next bulo, the numuke held the flintlock of his gun to the powder on the floor and fired. There was a great explosion, and all who were there died together— Da Monzon's soldiers and Mamari's favorite wife, his djeli and his numuke.

The people who were captured in Chiaro were driven to Da Monzon's camp, and Da Monzon spoke roughly to them as if they were already slaves. Mamari's son was among them, and he came forward and addressed Da Monzon, speaking through the king's djeli. He said, "Da Monzon, king of all Segu, you are great and your Tonjon is great. Yet if one river is larger than another, that does not mean its water is sweeter. We whom you have conquered are nobles, just as you who have conquered us are nobles. My father and your father worked together to create and preserve the kingdom of Segu. Though we lived here in Chiaro, we are all freeborn Bambara. When my father came to you in the capital he came in trust because of his great respect for you. He honored you in his words and actions. In my childhood and youth I never heard him say anything but good about your father and you. We do not deserve to be treated as slaves. As long as Segu lives, we ought to be considered free." When Da Monzon heard the young man speak so openly and without fear he said, "Aaah! Does he know he is talking to the king?"

Da Monzon's djeli said to him, "Great Da Monzon, what you have done to Chiaro will always be remembered in the songs of the djeli. What you do now to these people of Chiaro also will be recalled. Remember that they are not Fula or Manding or Maraka. They are Bambara, they are true citizens of Segu. If you are harsh with them, the ngoni of the djeli will speak of it. If you are generous with them, the ngoni of the djeli will speak of it. The ngoni retains everything. It is like a treasure chest from which nothing is ever lost. Everything that happens in the world is stored in the ngoni, and when a djeli plays this instrument he only liberates what is stored there. If you can be generous to these people of Chiaro, be generous. If you cannot, then it is destiny that you cannot."

Da Monzon was moved by the words of his djeli. He said, "I swore to the Twelve Fetishes of Segu that I would raze Chiaro, and this I must do. But these people can go elsewhere, and I will give them land to build a new town." So Chiaro Mamari's son and the other captives were set free.

But as for the city named Chiaro, Da Monzon ordered it destroyed. It ceased to exist, and in time there was nothing there but land covered with grass and other wild things.

Mamari's body was never found, and Da Monzon could not take his head back to Segu as a trophy of war. This is what Da Monzon's practitioners of the mystic sciences had prophesied, and Da Monzon said of them, "Their divinations spoke truly."

SEKURUNA TOTO'S PROPOSAL TO DA MONZON

O NE OF THE KINGDOMS THAT KING Da Djera had never been able to subjugate was Sekuruna, whose king was named Toto or Toto Koro. As ruler of Sekuruna, he was generally called Sekuruna Toto. He was very prosperous, and the djeli sang many praise songs extolling his wealth. It was a subject of which he never tired. His djeli sang:

> To have many horses makes you a rich man.
> To have many cattle makes you a rich man.
> To have much gold makes you a rich man.
> Sekuruna Toto, you are indeed a rich man.

It is said that whenever Sekuruna Toto heard this song he always became very happy and stood up and danced the king's dance. When

95

Da Djera became ill and felt that he was soon to die, he made his son Da Monzon promise that he would conquer Toto and bring his head to Segu. But years went by and Da Monzon did not attack Sekuruna because he did not have a clear-cut provocation from Toto. Finally it was Toto who provoked the war between the two kings.

Toto sent an emissary with an insult for Da Monzon. The message was that Toto had heard that Da Monzon was a very beautiful woman and he would like to have her for his wife. It clearly meant that Toto regarded the king of Segu as a weak and harmless person, even though Da Monzon considered himself to be a great hero. Da Monzon was about to reply angrily, but his counselors said to him, "No, do not give an abusive answer. It will only make Toto feel pleased with himself. Speak as he speaks and play the game with him." So Da Monzon told the emissary, "Thank Toto for us. We have heard his offer. Please tell him that Da Monzon's family must be consulted. If the family agrees, we will let you know and you can send the marriage payment."

The emissary returned to Sekuruna and reported to Toto. Some days after that, Da Monzon sent one of his djeli to Toto with the message, "Yes, Da Monzon's family consents, so you can give me the marriage payment and I will take it back to Segu." Toto ordered the marriage payment brought out and displayed before Da Monzon's djeli. It consisted of all the usual items—cloth, kola nuts, chickens and other such things. The djeli accepted the marriage payment and returned to Segu. When some time had passed, Da Monzon again sent his djeli to Sekuruna Toto to tell him, "The family of Da Monzon sends you greetings. The girl is mature now and ready to become a woman. The family wants to know when you would like to have her brought to you here in Sekuruna?" And Toto said, "Aaah! That is good, I would like to have her brought not this Friday, not next Friday, but on the third Friday. That is to say, in twenty-one days."

Now, all these exchanges between Da Monzon and Sekuruna Toto were in reality not an idle game, but a metaphor created out of Toto's original insult. When Toto said the girl should be brought in twenty-one days he was really saying that Da Monzon should bring his army in twenty-one days and begin the fighting. So Da Monzon began at once to prepare for his expedition. He ordered all his practitioners of the mystic sciences, both Bambara and Muslim, to do the usual things to make his fighters invulnerable to spears and bullets. And on the twenty-first day Da Monzon took his army to Sekuruna.

Sekuruna was strong. It had valiant fighters, and Toto also had morikes and filelikelas to give them protective magic. His soldiers stood off Da Monzon's army for many days. But whenever Da Monzon lost a thousand men, another thousand would come from Segu to replace them. In time the contest developed into a siege, with Da Monzon's fighters outside the walls and Toto's fighters within. Sekuruna was besieged for six months, and finally the city fell. Toto was captured and brought to Segu for execution. Before he died, the djeli of Segu sang to him:

> You boast of yourself, you boast.
> If a small man talks big,
> The king of Segu will make him a slave.
> Toto, Da Monzon uses you for money to buy wine.
> You said you were something, now you are nothing.

Da Monzon's war against Sekuruna Toto was not the last of the wars. He sent emissaries to one city and another demanding submission to Segu. Usually the cities submitted, but if a king refused to acknowledge Segu's supremacy, Da Monzon sent an expedition to conquer him. It was this way until there were no more kingdoms or cities to fight. Da Monzon controlled everything within reach, and finally the wars ended and the Tonjon had no more fighting to do. There were seven years of total peace under Da Monzon.

It is said in the songs of the djeli that the men of the Tonjon became restive when there was no more fighting to do. In frustration the tonjons pointed their guns at the sky and called to the sky people to come down and fight them. Other kings of Segu came and departed, but it was under Da Monzon that Segu was greatest. In the capital city the people prospered and there was something for everyone. Every man was busy doing his own work and leading his own life according to the talents and skills with which he had been endowed. Numukes forged iron and wrought in gold and silver, garankes tanned hides and made leather wares, farmers tilled the earth and harvested beyond the city walls, traders came and went, and proudly dressed heroes rode through the streets.

THE EPIC OF BAKARIDJAN KONE, A HERO OF SEGU

THE HEROES OF SEGU WERE NUMEROUS, and whenever they performed brave deeds they were praised in song by the bards. No man could achieve greatness and honor without some djeli composing poems about him that would make him remembered in generations to come. In the time of King Da Monzon there rose a hero named Bakaridjan Kone, who aspired only to a courageous and chivalrous life. He never sought power in Segu. He wanted only to demonstrate his valor, his skill, his generosity and his good character. Da Monzon was not always good to Bakaridjan, because he was jealous of his greatness. Yet Bakaridjan was always faithful to the king and to Segu. Even while he was still young, the djeli sang in his honor:

> There is only a single moon in the sky,
> But next to it there shines a brilliant star.

99

It meant that no one could compare with the king, but that Bakaridjan, as well as Da Monzon, cast his light over the kingdom.

This is the story of Bakaridjan Kone, how he came to Segu City, how he survived conspiracies against him, and how he earned honor and merit in the history of the kingdom of Segu.

Before Bakaridjan was yet born, his father lived with two wives in the village of Diosoro Nko, not far from Segu City. He was a freeborn noble, but he did not have noble pride in the conduct of his life. He was diffident in the way he cared for his two wives and his fields. He often thought, "Why am I living in Diosoro Nko? If I were in the capital city my life would be good."

This man from Diosoro Nko who was discontented with his life said over and over again, "Working in the fields is a burden, and there are no rewards. I will go to Segu City. Da Monzon has something for everyone. He is the owner of everything. It is said that if a man stands in the king's shadow good fortune comes to him." Finally, one morning, he announced to his wives that he was going to Segu City.

They asked him, "Who will take care of us?" He replied, "Life will go on." He left them to fend for themselves as though they had no husband. He went to Segu City. He arrived, he saw things happening, but gold did not rain down on him. He thought, "I will get close to Da Monzon and stand in his shadow. Then things will be good."

Every morning Da Monzon met with his advisers and Segu's notables in a large bulo, or anteroom, of his compound. The people assembled there to hear his pronouncements or his judgments in legal disputes. Behind the king were his counselors, and a djeli stood at his side. If there was a visitor from another city, he would announce himself through the djeli. If a chief brought taxes from a certain village, he would inform the djeli. Whatever business a person had with Da Monzon, he would speak to the djeli and the djeli would transmit the message to the king. Now, among those present in the assemblage every day were many who had no particular affairs to call to the king's attention. They simply sat before the king and acclaimed his decisions and judgments. Whenever the king made a pronouncement they would exclaim, "Oh, yes! Our king has spoken wisely!" or perhaps, "Da Monzon is right! His words are just!" It made no difference whether the king had spoken momentous or trivial words, these men praised him loudly. And when the day's assembly was over, Da Monzon had leavings of his meal brought to them, and he also gave them a few cowries.

The man from Diosoro Nko, he who was to be Bakaridjan's father, joined the chorus of praisers in Da Monzon's court. Like the others, he received food and cowries, and in this way he lived without exerting himself. Whether the king's words were right or wrong, he always exclaimed with the others, "Right!" Now, at the time he left Diosoro Nko, one of his wives, named Kumba, was pregnant. After some months, a traveler from his village brought the message that his wife had given birth to a male child. But the child's father did not go home because he was satisfied with being where he was. It was his duty to be in Diosoro Nko for the naming ceremony, but he did not want to give up his place in the king's morning assemblage.

However, in the hope of receiving a gift of some kind he made it known to the king through the djeli that he was the father of a newborn male child. Though the man from Diosoro Nko was a noble, and though he was a constant member of the praising chorus in the court, in Da Monzon's eyes he had sacrificed his prestige by doing what he was doing. Da Monzon considered him less than noble. He did not give him anything at all. Instead, he sent a messenger to visit Kumba and her co-wife, Jeneba. The messenger said, "Da Monzon has heard about your newborn son. He has heard about your difficulties. Therefore, he sends you these cowries so that you can conduct a proper naming ceremony. Da Monzon would like you to name the boy Bakaridjan." The naming ceremony was carried out and the boy was named according to the king's wishes.

Kumba and Jeneba were close friends, though this was not always the way it was with co-wives. They aided each other in everything and took care of Bakaridjan as if they had both given birth to him. Bakaridjan looked to them both as mothers, and to the end of his life he called himself the son of Kumba and Jeneba.

Da Monzon had many wives, but years passed and he had no children. One day he sent for a famous morike, Dukuba Almami, and said, "I am king of all Segu, yet I have no child. What is to be done?" The morike examined pages in the Koran, and he divined with kolas. When he was finished with the divining he said, "Great

101

king of Segu, an evil force stands in the way of your having children. But if you do as I tell you, the force will be broken. All of your wives are Bambara. If you conceive a child first with a Fula woman, your wives also will become pregnant." Da Monzon followed the advice of Dukuba Almami. He found a Fula woman he liked and had intercourse with her. She became pregnant and had a male child. In gratitude, Da Monzon made her one of his wives, and she came to live in the royal household. Soon the king's other wives became pregnant and had children, twelve of whom were males. All this happened about the time that Bakaridjan was born.

As Da Monzon watched his children grow, he began to wonder which of his sons would succeed him when he died. It was a time of great heroes in Segu. Champion fighters rode this way and that way across Segu to test their valor against other champions and thus achieve fame. Some passed through Segu City looking for contests with other heroes. The names of many heroes were heard in the songs of the djeli. Da Monzon began to ponder whether one of these heroes might not try to take power in Segu. It troubled his sleep. And so one day he sent for his morike, Dukuba Almami, and said to him, "I have called you because something troubles my sleep. When the light fades for me, one of my sons should be king of Segu. There are great heroes in Segu. But I do not fear that any of them will come to have a name equal to mine, but I want to know whether there is someone somewhere whose name will become more famous than all the others. If so, I must know who he is. If I know my enemy I can deal with him."

Dukuba Almami consulted his Koran. He divined with kolas. After that he said to Da Monzon, "Great king of Segu, the name of the person is not revealed to me. Yet this much I can tell you: He is not among the old men of Segu. He is not among the young men of Segu. He is to be found among the boys of Segu. That is where you must look." Da Monzon exclaimed, "Aaah! You speak in mysteries. If we do not know his name or where he lives, how will we ever know him if we see him?" Dukuba Almami consulted his kolas again. He said, "One by one you must call every boy in Segu to hold the stirrup of your horse while you mount. As you rise into your saddle, brace the point of your spear against the boy's foot, thus wounding him. An ordinary boy will cry out in pain or protest, or let go the stirrup and run away altogether. If you find someone who does not cry out or protest in any way, you will know that he is destined to become a hero so great that he might take Segu away from you."

Da Monzon said, "Yes, I will do it." And because he trusted that one of his own sons would succeed him, he put his own children to the test first. He called his oldest son and instructed him to hold the stirrup of the horse while he mounted. As Da Monzon rose in the stirrup he pressed the point of his spear against the boy's foot and put his weight on the shaft. The boy called out, "Oh, my father! You have pierced my foot!" And he let go of the stirrup and ran away, crying, "My father! You have wounded me with your spear!" Da Monzon said, "My son, it was an accident. Go and have your foot bound up." The king called another of his sons, then another, and it was the same with all of them. After that he tested all the boys of Segu in the same manner, and each one cried out and ran.

Da Monzon became frustrated. He said to his counselors, "Aaah! In this world you cannot believe anybody. My morike divined falsely. I gave him gold for his divination, but what he told me was not true." But one old man among the counselors was not afraid to argue with Da Monzon. He said, "Great king of Segu, for many years you were without any children. Then Dukuba Almami performed rituals for you. He exercised mystic powers that made it possible for your wives to conceive and bear. He did not deceive you. Let us consider the way things are. He said the person you are looking for is to be found among the boys. There are still other boys in Segu who have not yet been tested. Do you remember that some time ago you gave the name Bakaridjan to the child of Kumba and Jeneba, who live in Diosoro Nko? Did you test this boy also?"

Da Monzon answered, "Oh, yes, he was the first one. I came into the street and I met him, and I said, 'Come and hold my stirrup for me.' He came and held the stirrup and I wounded his foot with my spear. He could not endure it and ran away crying." Now, no man could tell the king, "You are saying what is wrong," because it would be taken as an insolent offense. But there was a way of saying this that was acceptable. A person would say, "Great king, it is something to laugh at." And this is what the old counselor said, "Da Monzon, what I have heard is something to laugh at." Da Monzon replied, "What I said is true. I met him, he held my stirrup and he ran away." Again the old counselor said, "Great king, it is something to laugh at. Bakaridjan does not live in the city, but in the village of Diosoro Nko. It must have been someone else." Da Monzon grew angry. He said, "Very well, I will send for Bakaridjan. When he arrives I will ask him in public whether or not I met him. If he says yes, then you will have made a mortal mistake that you will regret." The old counselor replied, "Yes, Da Monzon, let it be that way. I have lived a long time already and I can afford it."

So the king sent one of his slaves to the village of Diosoro Nko to find Bakaridjan and bring him to Segu. The slave went there, to the house of Kumba and Jeneba, and he found Bakaridjan lying outside on a mat. The slave greeted him. Bakaridjan replied, but he did not say, as a child should, "Good morning, father." Instead, he spoke an adult insult, saying, "Maharaba." The slave was startled. He said, "What manner of speaking is this? A small ragged boy like you speaks as though he were a village elder." Again Bakaridjan said, "Maharaba." The slave said, "Boy, whoever you are, I came here to find Bakaridjan. Where is he?" Bakaridjan said, "Why do you want Bakaridjan?" The slave answered, "The king sent me to get him." Bakaridjan said, "Aaah! What would the king of Segu want with a poor boy like Bakaridjan?" The slave became annoyed with Bakaridjan's manner. He said, "You small dirty boy in rags, what affair is it of yours? Why do you talk to me as if you were some kind of grand personage? Have you seen Bakaridjan or not?" Bakaridjan said, "Yes, he was nearby not long ago."

The slave began to call out, "Bakaridjan! Bakaridjan!" Bakaridjan said, "There is no use shouting like that. Go back to Segu and tell the king that Bakaridjan is coming." The slave answered, "Small boy, do not put your mouth in my story again." And he continued calling for Bakaridjan. Bakaridjan said to him, "Old man, go back and tell Da Monzon what I said. When Bakaridjan returns I will tell him the king wants him." The slave lost his temper. He said, "Shall I have to beat you for your impertinence?" He seized Bakaridjan, but because the boy was so thin he could not find a place to strike him. At last he hit the boy's distended stomach. Bakaridjan stood up in anger. He picked up his bush knife and approached the man as if to kill him. The slave turned and ran in fear, even though he had not found what he had come for.

He ran all the way to the city, and when he arrived at Da Monzon's house he was panting from the exertion and also from fear. The king asked him, "Well, did you locate Bakaridjan?" The slave answered, "Papapapa, yes, he is coming." The king thought, "He comes running and saying 'papapapa.' That must mean that Bakaridjan gave him a small lesson." A short while later Bakaridjan arrived. He greeted the people in words that only an elder person would use, like a hero addressing ordinary men. They spoke to him as to a child, but he answered in the language of an esteemed personage. All they could say in response was, "We hear it from you," meaning that they disbelieved what they heard.

Bakaridjan arrived at Da Monzon's court, where all the notables were gathered to witness the outcome. The king asked, "Bakaridjan, were you or were you not at my gate when I came out? Did we or did we not meet?" Bakaridjan answered, "Great king, no, you did not see me. The last time I was in Segu City was nine months ago during a festival. Your children were feasting and they invited me to eat with them. I took a little meat with my fingers and put it in my mouth. Then I stood up, saying I was satisfied. I went away, and when I was some distance from your house I spat out the meat because my stomach was not accustomed to such rich food. Since that day nine months ago I have not been in Segu."

What Bakaridjan said proved that the king's old counselor was right, that Da Monzon was wrong in saying that he had met the boy and tested him. To be proved wrong in public was embarrassing for the king. He directed his feelings toward Bakaridjan, saying, "You are a stupid boy. Look at yourself. See how skinny and dirty you are. Look at the rags you wear for clothes. You don't resemble your father in any way. He comes to my court. I give him food and cowries. He is fat. He is clean. But you, you make no effort. And the food my children give you, you spit it out."

As Da Monzon spoke to him in this way, tears came to Bakaridjan's eyes. He replied to the king with a proverb: "To be weak transforms an insult into a joke." It meant that an ordinary person could not defend himself against the unjust words of a king, and that witnesses to the insult could only laugh because the king had spoken. Bakaridjan said, "Great Da Monzon, if I had known that you wanted me here so you could make me look small in front of the nobles of Segu, I would not have come." He turned away and started to leave the assemblage.

Da Monzon called him back, saying, "Ééé! Bakaridjan, where are you going? You are my child, I gave you your name. I am entitled to make little jokes with you. Come back. I had a purpose in sending for you." Bakaridjan came back. The king said, "There is something I want you to do. I want you to help me mount my horse." So they went out together and Bakaridjan held the iron stirrup for the king. As Da Monzon set his foot in the stirrup, he placed the point of his spear on Bakaridjan's foot. As he raised himself into the saddle he bore down on the spear. Though his foot was pierced by the point, Bakaridjan made no sound. The king said, "Bakaridjan, I did not do it right. I must come down." He dismounted, pressing down again on his spear. Not a sound came from Bakaridjan's mouth. He did not move from where he was holding the stirrup. Da Monzon said, "I will try again," and he mounted once more, throwing more weight on his spear. Still there was no sign from Bakaridjan. When Da Monzon descended he saw that the spear point had penetrated Bakaridjan's foot, and he knew that he had found the person described in the morike's divination. This small boy, undernourished and ragged, was the one destined to have a great name in Segu.

Da Monzon said in feigned surprise, "Oh, Bakaridjan, what has happened? What is it with your foot? It is bleeding. Did I cut you with my spear?" Bakaridjan answered, "Great king of Segu, it does not matter. Whatever the king does, I will not complain." They went back to the royal house. When the people saw Bakaridjan walking with a bleeding foot, leading the king's horse, they were silent. They knew that a great event had occurred. Only Bakaridjan's father had anything to say. He said, "Aaah! This crazy boy is my son. He is stupid. He did this to himself. If he were not so stupid he would not have allowed himself to be injured this way." People standing nearby said, "Man, it is not the boy who is stupid but you. You do not understand what you are seeing."

The king ordered a slave woman to prepare a dressing for Bakaridjan's foot. She boiled oil until it was the consistency of butter and brought it in a pot. She set it down to cool, so that she could apply it to the wound. But Da Monzon was deeply disturbed that this boy was destined to become a great hero in Segu, and he ordered

Bakaridjan to place his wounded foot directly into the hot oil. Bakaridjan did what he was told to do. He remained silent and did not flinch. After that, the slave woman bound up his wound.

A dark shadow fell over Da Monzon's spirit. Now that he had found out for certain what he wanted to know, he realized that he could not let Bakaridjan go back to Diosoro Nko, but would have to keep him in the capital city where he could be watched. He sent a message to the boy's mothers, Kumba and Jeneba, to tell them that Bakaridjan would remain with him in his service. He said to the boy, "Bakaridjan, you are going to live here in the royal compound, and you will be treated as one of my children." But in the secret part of his mind he thought, "Something will have to happen to this boy before he attains his manhood."

One morning Da Monzon was sitting in the first of the six anterooms that led to his private quarters. He could hear his twelve sons playing games outside. Bakaridjan was not playing with the other children. He was sitting on a hide behind the king. It happened that the king's sons came running into the room, and when Da Monzon saw them his heart felt bitter because he was certain that none of them was destined to have a great name. He said, "My children, you see this poor boy, Bakaridjan, sitting behind me. His name will be a rising star in Segu. That is what the morike said, and his words are to be believed. I had hoped that one of you would become the paramount hero of Segu, but the kolas say it will be Bakaridjan." Da Toma, the king's eldest son, looked at Bakaridjan and said, "My father, do not worry about it. This skinny boy will never live to be remembered in Segu. I swear that we will not allow it."

When Bakaridjan heard these words he put his lips between his teeth and bit them. After the king and his children left the room, one of the king's djeli saw him sitting in this fashion and asked him, "My son, grandson of so-and-so, why are you crying?" That the djeli addressed him as "grandson of so-and-so" meant that he recognized Bakaridjan's noble lineage, even though the boy's father had demeaned himself by becoming a supplicant hanger-on at the court. The djeli named Bakaridjan's noble ancestors. He said, "The history of your family is well known. It had many heroes. Therefore, do not cry because the king wounded your foot and put it in hot oil."

Bakaridjan answered, "No, great djeli, it is not because of those things. It is because the king's eldest son, Da Toma, pledged to his father to kill me. I have not done anything. I lived in my village quietly, disturbing no one. The king had me brought here, though I did not want it. He tells his children that I will prevent them from having illustrious names. So Da Toma says, 'This skinny boy will never live to be remembered in Segu,' and the king is silent. What kind of place is Segu? Great djeli, do one thing for me. Tell Da Toma I will never forget the pledge he made to kill me."

Time passed. Bakaridjan's foot was not yet entirely healed. One day the king's sons asked their father for sickles so they could go into the bush and cut grass for the horses. Da Monzon ordered a slave to bring them sickles, and they departed. When they were gone, Bakaridjan also asked for a sickle so that he could cut grass, and he went out into the bush where the brothers were working. When it was time to bring the bundles of grass home, the king's eldest son said, "Bakaridjan, don't bother to put your bundle on your head. We are going to fight and I am going to kill you." Bakaridjan said, "No, I am not yet ready to fight. My foot has not healed." Da Toma said, "If you do not fight, I will tie you up and beat you until you die." Bakaridjan replied, "That is the way it is in the world of Segu. A rich man can abuse a poor man, and a rich man's son can abuse a poor man's son." Da Toma ordered his younger brothers to tie Bakaridjan's hands and feet. He ordered them to get sticks. He ordered them to beat Bakaridjan. Only the youngest of the brothers, Lakare, objected. He said, "This is not honorable. It is not right for twelve noble boys to beat someone who is helpless." Da Toma said, "Be silent. I am the one who says what shall be done." So they beat Bakaridjan until he lost consciousness. Believing that he was dead, they covered his body with leaves and returned home.

But Bakaridjan was not dead. After a while he crawled out from under the leaves and came back to the city. His body was bruised and bleeding. Da Monzon said, "Bakaridjan, what happened?" Bakaridjan answered, "Great king, do not be concerned. I merely fell among the thorns." Da Monzon said, "My son, you must take more care. It is better to come home without any grass than to be injured this way." Bakaridjan said, "Great king, it would have been shameful for me to return with nothing."

The next day was the same as the first. Bakaridjan went to where the king's sons were gathering grass, and again they beat him and left him for dead. But Bakaridjan revived and returned home. Again the king asked him what had happened, and he said, "Nothing." In the secret hiding place in his mind, Da Monzon understood what had occurred, but he said nothing. Once more, on the third day, the brothers beat Bakaridjan and once more he returned. This time the king said "Aaah!" But he did not ask any questions.

The following morning Bakaridjan did not go out for the grass gathering. Instead, he went to the quarter of the city where the blacksmithing was done, and he sat on the ground near a certain numuke. He did not say anything, but if the numuke needed something Bakaridjan brought it to him, and sometimes he worked the bellows to keep the fire hot. At last the man took notice of Bakaridjan by saying, "My son, I do not understand why you have been sitting here all day. What is it you want from me?" Bakaridjan answered, "My father, I want you to make a knife for me the length of my arm." The numuke said, "Why were you silent all day? I could have made the knife by now." Bakaridjan answered, "My father, when I came I found you busy with your work. I did not want to be disrespectful by interrupting you. So I had patience. I thought, 'A time will come when he will ask me, and then I will tell him.'" The numuke exclaimed, "Aaah! You are an exceptional boy. I will make the knife for you now." He made the long knife for Bakaridjan and would not take any payment for it. Bakaridjan said, "My father, I will remember your generosity."

Using the quill of a feather for a needle, Bakaridjan sewed a scabbard to hold the knife, and after that he returned home. He went to his mat and slept. In the morning he joined the king's sons where they were gathering grass. And when the cutting and bundling were done, as before, they prepared to beat him. But he said, "No, today it is finished. Three times you tried to kill me. I am not a slave. I refuse to accept anymore what you have been doing to me. Because you are sons of the king, that does not make you more noble than I. You, Da Toma, you are yearning to be some kind of a hero. But a hero does not lead a mob against a single adversary, he fights one to one. I have never done anything to injure you, yet you want to see blood flow. Let your younger brothers stand to one side.

You and I will fight without weapons. Whoever wins may kill the other." Da Toma said, "Yes, Bakaridjan, I accept, and I will give your blood to the Twelve Fetishes."

The two boys came together and fought hand to hand. Da Toma was the taller of the two. Several times he grasped Bakaridjan and tried to throw him to the ground, but Bakaridjan remained on his feet. They twisted, turned, struggled. The fighting went on a long time. Da Toma was becoming tired. He called out to his brothers, "Come and help me." But the youngest brother, Lakare, answered, "No, we are nobles. You must fight with honor, man to man. If you defeat Bakaridjan, then it is over. If Bakaridjan defeats you, then the second of us will fight him, then the third, but it must be honorably done." So Da Toma had to continue alone. He became exhausted, and when Bakaridjan threw him to the ground he was unable to get up. Bakaridjan took his long knife from its scabbard and killed Da Toma. He rubbed Da Toma's blood on himself. Turning toward the other brothers, he said, "Which of you will be the next to die?" When they saw Bakaridjan with Da Toma's blood smeared on him they became terrified and fled. As it was said, "The bush became too small for them." They ran one way and another in fright. They arrived in the city and each went to hide in the house of his mother.

Da Monzon saw the boys running. He called them together and asked, "What has happened? Why are you in a frenzy?" They answered three times to emphasize the truth of what they were saying: "Bakaridjan has killed Da Toma! Bakaridjan has killed Da Toma! Bakaridjan has killed Da Toma!" Da Monzon sent his guards into the bush, instructing them, "Find Bakaridjan and kill him. Let his body rot in the bush." The guards went out and saw Bakaridjan with his long knife, his face and body smeared with blood. Though they were brave fighters they became fearful. They said to one another, "Hold back! This fierce boy is protected by a jinn!" They backed away, and Bakaridjan returned to the palace by himself, his knife in his hand. Whoever saw him stood aside. Bakaridjan went through the first of the king's antechambers, then through the other five, and arrived at Da Monzon's private house. He entered and picked up Da Monzon's gun. It had magic power and could kill four men with one shot. After that he went out and faced the crowd that had gathered.

110

He ordered the king's guards to move to one side, and they did so. He ordered the king's sons to move to one side, and they did so. He held the king's gun ready to fire. Then one of the king's djeli spoke to him, saying, "Bakaridjan, what is it between you and your younger brothers?" For the djeli to speak this way was significant, because calling the king's sons Bakaridjan's younger brothers meant that he had earned seniority over them. Bakaridjan replied, "Let them tell you." The djeli said, "Yes, Bakaridjan, you are right. I will ask them." He asked one of the sons, and the boy replied, "I don't know. They were fighting, but I was not there. I did not see anything." The next son answered the same way, saying, "They fought in the bush, but I did not see it." All replied the same way until the djeli asked the youngest son, Lakare.

Lakare spoke honorably. He said, "My father, one day we came into your first antechamber and you said Bakaridjan was destined to become a paramount hero in Segu. Our eldest brother swore that he would kill Bakaridjan, and when he said those words Da Toma was already a dead person walking among the living." Da Monzon said, "Aaah!" Lakare continued, "Da Toma was determined to kill Bakaridjan. You did not say to him, 'No, it must not be done.' So when we went into the bush to cut grass Da Toma made us beat Bakaridjan until he was unconscious. We thought he was dead and covered him with leaves. We came home. But Bakaridjan was not dead. He also returned, and when you asked him why he was bloodied he said only, 'I fell among the thorns.' Did you not understand? For three days we beat Bakaridjan and tried to kill him because Da Toma ordered us to do it. After that, on the fourth day, Bakaridjan said, 'No, I will not suffer it again. I am a noble. I will fight you one to one, first the oldest, then the second oldest, down to the very last in the manner of honorable men.' Da Toma wanted us to come and help him, but we said, 'No, that is not the way of honor.' Bakaridjan threw him down and then killed him with his knife."

The king's counselors considered what they had heard. They said to Da Monzon, "Who can fault Bakaridjan? It was Da Toma who created the situation, and you did not discourage him." Though he was grieved by the loss of his eldest son, Da Monzon could not contradict anything that was said. He said, "Aaah, Bakaridjan, the

111

fault was not yours. My sons were wrong. Put down the gun. Nothing will happen to you. You acted honorably." Bakaridjan put down the gun. And because the king's words had been witnessed by the counselors, the djeli, the men of the Tonjon and many others, the affair was ended and Da Monzon was helpless to do anything to Bakaridjan.

Nevertheless, Da Monzon thought, "I cannot keep this boy here any longer. He has fire in his blood. Who knows what he will do?" So he decided to send Bakaridjan back to Diosoro Nko. He gave Bakaridjan a small horse and ordered his djeli to take him home. The djeli and Bakaridjan went to Diosoro Nko. Bakaridjan's mother, Kumba, exclaimed, "Aaah, Bakaridjan, you are here?" He said, "Yes, my mother, I am here." The king's djeli explained why the boy had been sent home, saying, "Bakaridjan behaved with great courage as a boy of noble birth should behave, and Da Monzon was pleased with him. But there was a fight and Bakaridjan killed the king's son. Therefore Da Monzon does not want him to live in the city anymore. That is the reason he is here."

When Kumba heard this she struck Bakaridjan. She said, "What a terrible thing you have done!" Bakaridjan spoke softly. He said, "My mother, you should not have struck me without hearing the story. You should know everything that happened. I will tell you how it was." He related the sequence of events, and after that she was penitent, saying, "My son, I am sorry I struck you. You were right in what you did."

In this way Bakaridjan returned to live in Diosoro Nko. But Da Monzon did not succeed in making him obscure, because even though Bakaridjan was not yet a man, people spoke of him with respect as a child-hero. Boys his own age came to Diosoro Nko seeking friendship with him, and in time they formed a fraternal club with Bakaridjan as their chief. They accepted his authority in all things. If Bakaridjan said, "Let us do something," they did it. The youth club's members were numerous, and even Bakaridjan did not know how many they were. So he let it be known that every member should bring a small stone and place it in a certain spot, and when that had been done he counted the stones and found that there were four hundred in all. They hunted and played at war together. They achieved prestige among the adults of Segu because of their numbers and because they were led by Bakaridjan.

One day Bakaridjan announced to them, "I am sending a message to Da Monzon to let him know we are ready to become men, and that we want the ceremony to take place in fifteen days." That was to say, the boys were setting a date for their circumcision. When Da Monzon received the message he was surprised, for matters of this kind were always decided by elders, not by children. He discussed the message with his counselors. They advised the king to agree to do whatever Bakaridjan wanted. They said, "Bakaridjan is not just an ordinary person. Our morikes tell us he is destined to greatness, and already there are some grown men who call him 'elder brother.' Let us do as he wishes." So Da Monzon ordered preparations to be made, and he instructed the numukes who would perform the circumcisions to be ready in fifteen days.

However, before the day of the circumcisions arrived, a large party of Fula from Massina launched a great cattle raid against Segu. They came in the night to Segu's cattle pens on the outskirts of the city, overcame the guards, and took all the cows, goats and sheep, driving them toward Massina. When the news was brought to Da Monzon, he announced a general mobilization. Messengers were sent to towns and villages. The king's orders declared that all able-bodied men should assemble in Segu with their weapons, young men, old men, and youths nearing the age of manhood.

Before dawn the next morning the streets of Segu were crowded with warriors, and other fighters were encamped outside the city walls. There were five thousand foot soldiers and one thousand horsemen. Knives and spears were sharpened, guns were readied, and blacksmiths repaired damaged weapons. The clamor drowned out the voices of the women in the marketplace, and the sound of pestles could not be heard. When Da Monzon gave the order, the army of Segu departed in pursuit of the Fula of Massina.

Bakaridjan was sleeping in his mother's house in Diosoro Nko on the morning of the military expedition. When his mother came to his room and saw him sleeping, she called out, "Bakaridjan! Bakaridjan! Why are you here? The fighters of Segu assembled in the city before dawn." Bakaridjan awakened. He said, "My mother, why are you disturbing my sleep?" She said, "The king's army has already gone out in pursuit of the Fula of Massina." Bakaridjan said, "My mother, do you own any cows, goats or sheep?" She answered, "No, I am very poor. I do not own any livestock." Bakaridjan said, "Then

113

why do you worry? The Fula did not take anything of yours. Da Monzon said for the men to come in the morning, but I am Bakaridjan and morning has not yet come for me." He went back to sleep.

When he was finished sleeping he arose, saying, "Now I am ready. Give me something to eat." After eating, he mounted the small horse the king had given him and rode to the city. When Da Monzon saw Bakaridjan arriving at the palace gate he reproached him. "Bakaridjan, my son, you are very late. The army is gone. I expected you to be here before any of the others." Bakaridjan replied, "My father, your orders said 'early morning.' What is early morning for some is not early morning for others. My early morning is now." Da Monzon said, "You are the leader of the boys' club that demanded to become men on a certain day. But your group has gone to war and you are still here. Where is your valor now?"

Bakaridjan said, "As you can see, now I am going to war. But the horse you gave me is too small. If I ride him into battle, any Fula I meet will be looking down and I will be looking up. I need a larger horse." Da Monzon said, "Aaah, my son, there are no horses here. All the horses are pursuing the Fula." Bakaridjan answered, "No, one horse remains, your djibedjan, the one you ride only at important festivals. Since you have no other horses, I will take your djibedjan." Da Monzon said, "Aaah!" No one but the king was allowed to ride the djibedjan. But he did not want to oppose Bakaridjan, so he ordered his grooms to bring the horse and saddle it. It was a fine, tall horse, and the bit in its mouth and the stirrups at its sides were made of silver. Bakaridjan mounted, saying, "Do not be concerned, you will see your horse again." He went as if to depart. But when Da Monzon was out of sight, Bakaridjan managed to find the king's spear, which could kill two men at one throw, and the king's gun, which could kill four men at one shot. He dropped them over the wall into the street, and when he rode out the gate of the compound he retrieved the two weapons. Then he went in pursuit of Da Monzon's army.

He traveled a great distance before he saw dust in the air stirred up by the feet of horses. Soon he came upon Da Monzon's army. It was not going toward Massina but returning to Segu. He said, "Are you coming back? I do not see the cattle." They answered, "No, we could not get the cattle. We caught up with the Fula and there was a great battle. We killed and they killed, but they are valiant fighters and we could not subdue them. There is nothing more to be done and so we are returning to Segu."

Bakaridjan had no intention of turning back, but he dissembled, saying, "Well, there is no use for me to go any further. If the heroes of Segu were not able to do anything, who can do it? So wait for me here. I must go into the bush to relieve myself. When I come back we will return to Segu together." He rode into the bush, and when they could no longer see him he turned and continued after the Fula. The others waited, and when Bakaridjan did not come back they said, "The boy is making fools of us. He is hiding in the bush. Let us go home." They did so, and when they were at last in Segu they reported to Da Monzon that they had been defeated. The king said, "Èèèèh! This is very bad news. All of the city's cattle are gone, our cows, our sheep, our goats. In addition, I have lost my djibedjan, my special spear and my special gun." They told Da Monzon, "We met Bakaridjan on the way. He went into the bush and we never saw him again." The king replied, "Aaah! Can he be the one who is supposed to have a great name in Segu?"

As for Bakaridjan, he followed the trail of the Fula toward Massina. Just as daylight was fading he caught sight of them in the distance, and he approached cautiously. They were preparing to camp for the night. They had traveled far from Massina to Segu, taken the cattle, journeyed, fought a battle and journeyed again, driving the cattle before them. Now they were tired. They ate their food and lay on the ground to sleep, their horses tethered nearby. When their campfires were burned out, Bakaridjan dismounted and crept into their midst. First he untethered their horses and led them away. Then he reentered the camp and stood amid the sleeping men in the darkness. He fired two shots from the king's gun and ran among the Fula shouting, "The Bambara are here! The Bambara are here!" The Fula leaped to their feet and searched for their horses, which were not there. They ran this way and that, not knowing what they were doing, or who were their fellow Fula. They wielded their spears and fired their guns. Fula fought Fula, and many were killed or wounded. At last the Fula chief became convinced that their situation was hopeless, and he went out of the camp and stood on a small hill, shouting, "Wooooo! Massina! Massina!" Hearing his voice the Fula fled from the encampment and joined him. Together

115

they left the place and began to make the return journey to Massina. They said to one another, "Those Bambara fighters must have great supernatural powers, else how could they come upon us without our horses whimpering?" When the sun rose they discovered that only forty of their men out of an army of four hundred had survived.

Bakaridjan drove all the cattle, sheep and goats back to Segu, and also the horses of the Fula. He was welcomed with dancing and singing in the streets, and even Da Monzon stood at his gate and performed a king's dance. No one contested that Bakaridjan was a true hero of Segu, and those who had mocked him now were silent. He gave back to Da Monzon the horse, the gun and the spear he had borrowed, but the king was so elated that he gave the horse and silver stirrups to Bakaridjan as a present. The chief djeli of the court composed a song in Bakaridjan's honor:

> You, Bakaridjan, who had nothing,
> By your action you have earned everything.
> Many blows were struck against the Fula,
> But it was your blows that drove them to Massina.
> You who returned last from the fighting,
> It was you who gave us back our cattle.
> We know you now, Bakaridjan,
> You are a valorous hero of Segu.
> There can be only one moon in the sky,
> But next to it shines a brilliant star.

The day of the circumcisions arrived, and Bakaridjan, along with the others of his youth group, became men.

Let us remember that the times in which Bakaridjan was born were times of heroes. There were men who were born to be farmers or blacksmiths and there were men who were born to perform heroic deeds. This was the way that fate governed the universe. Each man had the mark of his future on him from the beginning, and his life stretched ahead of him like a road from which he could not turn. Bakaridjan was great because he was destined to be great. He suffered the pain of the king's spear in his foot without making a sound. He took abuse from the king's sons when he had no choice, and then by all the rules of honor he killed Da Monzon's eldest son. And single-handed, when Segu held him in ridicule, he attacked four hundred Fula from Massina and destroyed them.

Though he was still young, he was now consulted by the old men on tactics of war. When there was fighting to be done, Bakaridjan rode in front with the older heroes of Segu, and they respected him and gave him room to wield his weapons. Da Monzon gave him a battalion to command, and after that an army. Even when Segu was not threatened by invading Fula, Bakaridjan did not put his weapons down. He went out time after time to subjugate cities that had refused to acknowledge Da Monzon's authority. He expanded Da Monzon's kingdom for him.

But even while Bakaridjan did these things, and even while Da Monzon rewarded him with honors, the king remained uneasy. He thought of the djeli's song, "There can be only one moon in the sky, but next to it shines a brilliant star." He worried that the star might outshine the moon itself, and he sometimes could not sleep at night for thinking about Bakaridjan. One day he called his favorite morike, Dukuba Almami, and asked him if he could not employ the mystic sciences to prevent Bakaridjan from coming home from war. Dukuba Almami consulted his Koran and his divining kolas many times, but the answer was always the same: "Great king, Bakaridjan has within him a force that cannot be deflected. If you shoot an arrow at him it will turn aside as it approaches his body. A spear that strikes him will be blunted. A bullet fired at him will fall to the ground harmlessly. He is protected not only by the magic charms he wears, but by the force within his mind. His character is noble. He is relentless against an enemy, yet he is compassionate. If his enemy is afraid of him, Bakaridjan turns away without striking him. He will not fight a man of caste, but only a person as noble as himself. He is generous. He gives cowries, cattle or food to people who are in need. He does not amass his wealth, but shares it. He respects the old. He lives by the noble code of honor. His words are full of fire, yet he knows how to be gentle. Because he lives in honor his force is strengthened. Even though you fear him, there is no fault in him that gives you the right to kill him."

Da Monzon replied, "But I have many living sons. Surely one of them should rule Segu when the light has faded for me. Yet Bakaridjan shades them from the sun and they stand in his shadow." Dukuba Almami answered, "Great king, let your mind rest. Bakaridjan does not want to take your place. He wants only to be remembered for his valorous deeds and his services to Segu."

Bakaridjan went on with his conquests for Da Monzon, but there were times when all was quiet and there was no fighting in Segu. When the quiet became prolonged Bakaridjan felt restive. He would go to Da Monzon, saying, "Such and such a city is stubborn. It does not recognize Segu as paramount. I will go there and reason with the king." Da Monzon would say, "He has not done anything. Is there a provocation?" And Bakaridjan would answer, "When I arrive there I will find it."

He went one time to a certain city. He was greeted by the king, and he answered, "King, your name offends me. The name of your city offends me. They are bad names. Therefore I am here to make war on you." The king answered, "Bakaridjan, there is no reason to make war. If our names are so offensive to you, wait until tomorrow. I will shave my head." Now, on the seventh day of a baby's life its head was shaved and it was given its name. What the king was saying to Bakaridjan was, "Do not attack me because of my name. Tomorrow I will shave my head and take a new name that will please you." But Bakaridjan answered, "My father, it is too late for that. You are too old to shave off your hair. It is not your hair I want but your head." So there was a battle, and when Bakaridjan won he took the king's head back to Segu.

Bakaridjan brought many kings' heads to Da Monzon. He attacked Bassala and conquered it. He attacked Kankelema and conquered it. He attacked Sonsorubuqu and conquered it. He attacked Porige, Saribugu, Takuru, Galama and Nonobugo and conquered them. In all, Bakaridjan was victorious over more than twenty cities, and some djeli tell that the number was more than thirty. Through his efforts the power and authority of Segu expanded over a vast territory.

There is the world of the seen and the world of the unseen. Beneath the River Joliba, near the city of Bamako, there was a kingdom of water jinns, and its ruler was named Samarussi. Though they were not humans, the water jinns lived in the manner of humans. The ruler governed like a king of men. He had his court, his counselors, his blacksmiths and his slaves. But the water jinns were different from men in that they had extranatural powers. And they were different also in their appearance. While their bodies were dark, from foot to knee their skins were white, and their arms were white as well. They were formed like humans, except that their heads were triangular in shape. No human could see a jinn without recognizing him.

It happened that in this kingdom of water jinns there was one whose name was Bilissi. His behavior was brutal and uncivilized, and he continually offended his community in one way or another. He was arrogant toward the weak, ruthless toward women and contemptuous of honorable living. The jinns complained many times to their ruler, Samarussi, and at last Samarussi called a meeting of his counselors to discuss what should be done. It was decided that Bilissi would be exiled from the city of the jinns. He was called, and Samarussi informed him that he would have to leave or die. Bilissi said, "Where am I to go?" And Samarussi said, "Go above and live in the land of humans."

So Bilissi left the water and traveled northward along the River Joliba until he came to the capital of Segu. He made himself a house, settled, and went on living. His appearance in Segu made the people fearful, and they avoided him. His behavior above was as bad as it had been below. He was arrogant and ruthless to slaves and nobles alike, but no one dared to restrain him. The people called him Mangala Ntini, meaning Small God. Although he was sometimes called a hero, it was only because of his strength and supernatural powers, for he did not behave according to the code of true heroes.

It was the custom in Segu that every week a cow was killed for the heroes to share. It was called the Cow of Heroes, or the Meat of Heroes. Every man of great valor came and took a portion of the meat. Lesser men, even though they had been brave in combat, would not claim a portion. Those who shared the Cow of Heroes were expected to be in the forefront of every battle. When Bilissi

119

arrived in Segu, he came and demanded a portion of the cow. Every week he came and claimed it, and no one prevented him.

Because there was so much hostility against him in Segu, Bilissi went to stay in a small village not far from the city. But before he left he announced, "Though I am going to live outside the capital, I am not giving anything up. I will go when I please and come when I please. Whichever way I am going, do not block the trail, but stand aside. As to the Cow of Heroes, I do not relinquish my share. On the day the cow is killed I will be here to get my portion, because I am a hero beyond heroes in Segu. Whoever denies it, let him come and tell me. But if I am not here the day the cow is killed, leave my portion where it is and I will send for it when I am ready." So even though Bilissi might not be there to take his meat, no one appropriated it. Sometimes he did not claim it at all, and it lay on the ground to rot or be eaten by eagles and dogs.

Bakaridjan had been away on an expedition when Bilissi arrived in Segu. After his return he heard about him. He was angry to hear what had been going on. He said to Da Monzon, "Why has no one punished this person?" Da Monzon said, "Bakaridjan, what Bilissi is doing is bad. But he is not human, he is a water jinn. He has powers exceeding those of men. Neither spears nor bullets can penetrate his body. Do not provoke him. Let him be." Bakaridjan answered, "In this life everything good comes to an end and everything bad comes to an end. For each one of us there is an end, even for Small God. I will challenge him by taking his portion of the Cow of Heroes." Everyone protested, saying, "Bakaridjan, do not do it. Bilissi will kill you."

But Bakaridjan did not listen. When the next Cow of Heroes was killed, he took his own portion and he also took the part reserved for Bilissi. He ordered his slave to carry the meat away, but he himself remained behind and made conversation with other heroes of Segu. In time, Bilissi arrived. He said, "Who has taken my meat?" Bakaridjan answered, "I am the one." Bilissi said, "Aaah, young man, you have made a mistake. The meat is reserved for me." Bakaridjan answered, "As you can see, I did not reserve it. You, Bilissi, claim to be a hero. Any man can claim to be a hero, but what have you ever done for Segu that entitles you to make a claim? Have you ever fought with us against the Fula? Have you conquered any cities and put them under the protection of Da Monzon? And how have you demonstrated your honor? Have you been kind to helpless people? Do you show respect to old men? Do you give a little food to grandmothers who have no one to take care of them? Have you ever carried a bundle of wood for a cripple? Have you ever done anything in your life except abuse the weak?"

Bilissi said, "Your words are those of an innocent child. You do not know me or you would not speak this way. So give me the meat and we will let the matter rest." Bakaridjan answered, "Oh, yes, I know you, Bilissi. You are the one who comes from under the river and spoils our life in Segu. You will get no more meat here from the Cow of Heroes." Bilissi said, "Then you are confronting me?" Bakaridjan answered, "I am confronting you." Bilissi said, "Very well, let it be that way. Not this Friday, not the Friday after, nor the next, but on the fourth Friday we will meet outside the city walls. But what will you use for weapons? There is no spear or bullet that can pierce my body." Bakaridjan answered, "I have the weapon to kill you. The weapon is myself."

Bilissi returned to his village. He was certain of his own powers, but he wondered about the powers of Bakaridjan. There was a saying that whoever puts flour in his mouth must have the saliva to swallow it. Perhaps Bakaridjan had a mysterious strength in him.

After delivering his challenge to Bilissi, Bakaridjan went to an accomplished practitioner of the mystic sciences named Serible Karamoko, whose name meant Master Teacher from Serible. He said to Serible Karamoko, "Help me. I have to ask for your protection because I am going to fight Bilissi, the Small God." Serible Karamoko listened. He said, "My son, you are undertaking a very dangerous enterprise. You can capture a city, that is one thing. You can make a king into a slave, that is another thing. Yet to fight Bilissi is something extraordinary. Yet I will do what I can for you. Come back in three days and I will tell you what I have learned."

After Bakaridjan had left, Serible Karamoko, being a Muslim, said prayers to Allah. Then he perused the Koran, looking for guidance in its pages. He divined with kola nuts. And finally, using his powers of mystic communication, he sent words through space to Samarussi, ruler of the water jinns in the depths of the River Joliba. He invoked Samarussi, calling, "Samarussi! Samarussi! It is I, Serible Karamoko, in Segu. The matter is urgent." He continued his invocations without resting. His words reached Samarussi's ears. But Samarussi was trying to sleep, and the constant invocations disturbed him. He sent one of his messengers to Serible Karamoko's house to say, "My master, Samarussi, is trying to sleep. He requests that you stop your invocations, for you are disturbing him."

But the morike did not stop. He continued to send the words, "Samarussi! Samarussi! The matter is urgent." At last Samarussi gave in to Serible Karamoko's appeals. He sent messengers to bring Serible Karamoko to his house. They went above and took the morike under the river. Samarussi and Serible Karamoko sat on hides and discussed the matter of Bakaridjan and Bilissi. Samarussi said at last, "We exiled Bilissi because he defiled our way of good living. We did not intend him to make life miserable for humans. What Bakaridjan has undertaken to do is very difficult. I want to help you. But I need guidance from my elder brother, Sankamaro, who lives under the ocean. Wait for me here. I will consult with him."

Samarussi had the power of mystic travel, and he journeyed instantly to the place of his elder colleague, Sankamaro. After listening to Samarussi, Sankamaro said, "Here are four talismans. One is white, one is black and two are red. Give them to Bakaridjan, and instruct him this way: Bakaridjan must buy two rams, one white and one black. The white talisman must be placed around the white ram's neck, and that ram will be called Bakaridjan. The black talisman will be placed around the black ram's neck, and that ram will be called Bilissi. The two rams shall fight, and what they do will foretell the outcome of the contest between Bakaridjan and Bilissi. After that, every morning Bakaridjan will go in the bush and call, 'Bilissi! Bilissi! Bilissi!' Bilissi will answer, 'Yes! Yes! Yes!' Bakaridjan will say three times, 'Bilissi, I have you! Bilissi, I have you! Bilissi, I have you!' And Bilissi will answer, 'Yes, Bakaridjan, you have me.' As for the two red talismans, Bakaridjan will wear them, one in his pocket and one in his hat."

Samarussi returned to his place in the River Joliba. He told Serible Karamoko everything he had learned and gave him the talismans for Bakaridjan. The morike then went back to his own village. On the third day Bakaridjan came to his house, and Serible Karamoko informed him about everything. The morike said, "If you are to win this fight against Bilissi you must follow all the instructions given to me below the water. And there is still one more thing. Bilissi does not fight with a spear or gun, but with a garan. For most men, a garan is only the special rope with which they hobble their horses. Bilissi's garan has magical force. If he strikes a man with it, the man is finished. Stay out of range of Bilissi's garan. Spar, dodge and feint so that it does not touch you. If necessary, ride away." Bakaridjan said, "My morike, I hear you."

Bakaridjan bought a white ram and a black ram. Around the neck of the white one he tied the white talisman, and he called that ram Bakaridjan. Around the neck of the black one he tied the black talisman, and he called that ram Bilissi. He brought them together to fight. They fought all day. Toward evening the white ram turned away from the fight and ran, with the black one in pursuit. They ran a long time. The white one came to an old dry well and jumped across it. The black ram came to the dry well and jumped, but he fell into the well and died. Bakaridjan thought, "I begin to perceive."

The next morning Bakaridjan went out into the bush and faced Bilissi's village. He called out, "Bilissi! Bilissi! Bilissi!" Now, Bilissi's house was some distance away, but the red talismans that Bakaridjan carried in his pocket and his hat brought the sound of his voice to where Bilissi was eating his morning meàl. Bilissi answered, "Yes! Yes! Yes!" and the sound of his words was brought to where Bakaridjan was standing in the bush. Bakaridjan called out, "Bilissi, I have you! Bilsisi, I have you! Bilissi, I have you!" Bilissi's voice came back, "Yes, Bakaridjan, you have me."

The day of the fight arrived. The people of the city closed the gates so that neither fighter could run within the walls for sanctuary, and they stood on the rooftops to watch. Bakaridjan mounted his horse and waited. Bilissi came riding. He said, "My son, you are here." Bakaridjan said, "Yes, I am here." Bilissi did not carry a gun or a spear, only his magical garan. The two riders faced one another. Bilissi said, "Very well, young brother, you may try first." He removed his shirt and raised his arms, thus exposing his body. Bakaridjan fired his gun three times—kao! kao! kao!—but the bullets could not penetrate Bilissi's chest.

Bilissi said, "Aaah, you tried. Now it is my turn." He rode toward Bakaridjan, brandishing his garan. But Bakaridjan moved his horse quickly to one side and then another, and the garan did not touch him. Bilissi persisted, pressing as close as he could, until at last Bakaridjan rode his horse away rapidly. Bilissi followed him. People on the roofs in the city cried out, "Bakaridjan is fleeing." The two fighters raced through the bush, Bakaridjan in the lead, Bilissi behind. The people could see them going back and forth. The sun reached the middle of the sky. Still the fighters raced. The sun began to decline and still the race went on. In the late afternoon Bakaridjan's horse came to a dry well and leaped across. When Bilissi's horse reached the well it stumbled and fell in. Bilissi's bones were broken and he could not move, yet he lived.

Bakaridjan rode back to the well. He saw Bilissi lying there helplessly. Bilissi said to him, "My young brother, you are a brave and skillful fighter. No one else has ever dared to challenge me. Now you want my head for a trophy. You have earned it. But you cannot finish me off with your weapons. No iron can kill me. No bullet can kill me. The secret of my death is wood." Bakaridjan understood. He cut a limb from a tree and shaped it into a knife. He gave it a sharp point and a sharp edge. He returned to the dry well and killed Bilissi with it, and with the same wooden knife he cut off Bilissi's head.

He mounted his horse and rode back to the city. His body was covered with the dust of battle, and the people watching from the walls and the housetops could not discern who was approaching. Because they were convinced that Bilissi could never be defeated, they believed that it was he who was coming, not Bakaridjan. They jumped down in fear from the walls and the housetops and ran in all directions, seeking safety. Even the tonjons fled, rushing to the king's quarter of the city for asylum, pushing their way into the outer bulo of Da Monzon's residence. In the turmoil they knocked down one of the king's sons and trampled him so that he died.

Da Monzon asked, "What is the trouble? What is the cause of the panic?" Some answered, "The battle is over. Bilissi has won, he is coming to take revenge on Segu!" Some said, "It appears to be Bilissi, but we could not tell for certain because he and his horse are covered with dust!" Others said, "It is surely Bilissi, there is no doubt about it!" The conversation was agitated. Da Monzon did not see his son in the crowd, and he asked, "Where is my son who was playing outside the bulo?" They answered, "Aaaah, king, while we were running we saw your son on the ground." They spoke this way, indirectly, because Da Monzon always executed those who brought bad news to him. The king said, "You mean my son is dead!" The tonjons replied, "Aaaah! The king says his son is dead!" Because the king had spoken the words, they could not be held responsible for the bad news. They repeated, "The king says his son is dead!"

Bakaridjan sat on his horse before the main city gate, waiting to come in. The people refused to open the gate. Then Bakaridjan's son, Simbalan Kone, a boy who was not yet quite a man, called out, "Open the gate, it is my father, Bakaridjan." Still they would not do it. So Simbalan said, "Give me four brave tonjons and I will prove to you that Bilissi is dead." The king gave him four tonjons, and they went to the place where the battle had ended. There they found Bilissi's body and his severed head. Because Bilissi was a water jinn, his body was not like that of humans. The head was very heavy, and it took the four tonjons to lift it. They carried the head back to the city and the people saw it was Bilissi and not Bakaridjan who had been killed. They opened the gate and permitted Bakaridjan to enter. They cried out praises to Bakaridjan. Never before had there been such a victory. They celebrated. They feasted, drank wine and danced.

The king's djeli came to Bakaridjan's house and sang a praise song to him:

> Welcome, Bakaridjan.
> Bakaridjan, the gold drum is yours.
> Bakaridjan, he silver drum is yours.
> Bakaridjan, the djeli of Segu are singing your song.

The meaning of the song was that Bakaridjan was the greatest of all Segu's heroes.

Yet all was not well with Bakaridjan. Because Bilissi was a jinn he possessed great magical powers, and their effects did not die with him. Bakaridjan fell sick, and his body became paralyzed on one side. One arm and one leg were useless. He lay on his sleeping mat, unable to stand. When his son Simbalan Kone saw how things were, he went to Da Monzon and said, "Great king, Bilissi terrorized Segu for a long time. Even when he was dead the people were afraid to open the city gate. My father Bakaridjan has saved Segu from this terrible jinn. But now my father is sick with a great sickness given to him by Bilissi and cannot rise from his sleeping mat." Simbalan then spoke to Da Monzon in a way no person should address the king of Segu. He said: "Great king of the Four Segus, you are master of everything. The gold is yours, the cowries are yours, the cattle are yours and the land is yours. You are the master of everything. But I am Simbalan Kone, son of Bakaridjan. I am a freeborn noble, and so I am the master of my own life. Therefore I speak to you as one noble to another. I know you have always resented Bakaridjan and hoped to be rid of him. All Segu knows it. Nevertheless, Da Monzon, it is up to you to see that my father is cured. I will give you forty days to accomplish it. If Bakaridjan is not well in forty days, you will come to the end of your time."

When Da Monzon heard these words, anger overtook him. But because Bakaridjan had shown superhuman powers in killing Bilissi, the king thought, "Perhaps this boy also has superhuman strength." He said, "Simbalan Kone, do not be concerned. In forty days your father will be well again." When Simbalan was gone, the king sent for forty filelikelas, that is to say forty Bambara practitioners of mystic sciences. He said to them, "Bakaridjan killed Bilissi, but Bilissi's magic lingers on and Bakaridjan is paralyzed. It is up to you to make him well. Bakaridjan's son, Simbalan, has said that if it is not accomplished in forty days he will kill me. Perhaps he has the power to do it, I do not know. But I give you the same message. If you have not cured Bakaridjan in forty days you will all be killed and sacrificed to the Twelve Fetishes of Segu." The filelikelas answered, "Great king, do not be concerned about it. We will do our mystic work, and Bakaridjan will be well in forty days." They departed and began to gather herbs from the bush to make magic lotions for Bakaridjan.

Da Monzon then sent for forty morikes, Muslim practitioners of the mystic sciences. He spoke to them the same way. He told them that if Bakaridjan was not cured in forty days they would be killed and sacrificed to the Twelve Fetishes. They, also, assured the king that they could do what he wanted through their knowledge of divination and the Koran.

And so forty filelikelas and forty morikes worked day and night to accomplish the cure of Bakaridjan. Because they had profound knowledge they overcame the effects of Bilissi's magic, and before the forty days were up, Bakaridjan was well once more. Again he was seen in the streets of Segu. Again he rode his horse with silver trappings. Again he feasted and drank with other heroes. Again the celebrated djeli of Segu composed praise songs to him. Again, on special days, he sat in a prominent place in the king's court.

Yet it is said that to journey a great distance in the bush a person climbs hills and descends into gullies, and it is also said that although the moon throws its light on men, the moon is sometimes dark. Whatever destiny a person carries within him, there can be cruel moments as well as triumphs in his life.

Now, there was a beautiful young Fula woman in Segu by the name of Aminata, and Bakaridjan was "in conversation" with her. To be in conversation meant that a young man would have the special company of a young woman with whom he would spend his idle hours talking in friendship, without, however, making any sexual claims on her. Bakaridjan spent his evenings in Aminata's house, revealing his thoughts and listening to hers. Whenever he came to visit, she placed a mat on the floor for him and gave him a cotton blanket and a pillow. He would lie on the mat and she would sit on a nearby stool and they would converse.

But two other popular heroes of Segu, named Madiniko and Bamana Diase, also were in conversation with the Fula woman. Whenever they arrived at her house she would put down mats for them in different parts of the room and she would place her stool in the center. First she would converse with one of the men. Then, after a while, she would turn and talk to the second. Later, she would turn and make conversation with the third. When she spoke with one, the other two lay silently and did not interrupt, although each of them was resentful of the presence of the others. Day by day, evening by evening, the three men fell in love with Aminata. She understood what was happening, but she was fond of all three and did not resolve the competition by declaring a preference.

Many persons in Segu observed that the Fula woman was in conversation with Bakaridjan, Madiniko and Bamana Diase at the same time. They debated the virtues of the three heroes and recalled the accomplishments of each of them. They were less interested in the Fula woman's role in the affair than in which man would emerge as the supreme champion of Segu if it came to a challenge of honor among them. Some persons said, "Bakaridjan is the supreme hero of Segu." Some said, "Madiniko is the greatest of champions." And some said, "No, Bamana Diase has the greatest skill and valor."

A time came when Da Monzon heard of the debate. He asked questions and learned the whole story. He sent for his two chief djeli and said, "This matter between Bakaridjan, Madiniko, Bamana Diase and the Fula woman must be resolved. It is a bad situation. The heroes do not challenge one another. They are as docile as sheep. Let us find out which of them is superior to the others. You, my djeli, I put the matter in your hands. You must devise a competition among them that will settle everything. It is not good the way things are." The two djeli answered, "Great king, do not be concerned. We will do it."

In a small village not far from the city there was a celebrated hunter hero whose name was Dosoke Zan, meaning Zan the Hunter. He had never been defeated in battle. It was said that his mystic strength had been given to him by the chief of jinns, and for many years no hero seeking honor and valor dared to challenge him. The two djeli decided to test Bakaridjan, Madiniko and Bamana Diase against Zan the Hunter. In the evening the djeli went to Aminata's house. They found Aminata sitting on her stool and around her, in different parts of the room, the three heroes lying on their mats. The djeli sang a praise song to Aminata, after which she gave them some gold. They turned then to Bakaridjan and praised him, singing about his ancestors and the important things they had done. When they finished, they said, "Bakaridjan, we have something to tell you. All Segu knows that you, Madiniko and Bamana Diase have proven your valor in many great deeds. Everyone knows that you gather here in Aminata's house every evening to make conversation. They are saying, 'It is a strange thing that is happening. Usually one man and one woman are in conversation with each other. But in this case three great heroes come at the same moment.' People say, 'What kind of heroes are they who come together and share Aminata's time and attention? Are they afraid of one another? Perhaps they are not valorous at all. But if they are, which is the greatest of the three?' Segu wants to know which of you stands above the other two."

Bakaridjan replied, "Great djeli, do not bother about it. I will show you who is the greatest. Here, I make you a present of a large gift of gold, one portion for each of you. Now it can be said that Bakaridjan is the most generous of heroes." But the two djeli rejected Bakaridjan's gift. They said, "No, Bakaridjan, this is not what we want. We want to test your valor. We want you to bring us the gun of the famous Dosoke Zan." Bakaridjan answered, "Aaaah! Will a small thing like that satisfy you? Do not worry about it. I will bring you the gun." The djeli answered, "Bakaridjan Kone, we thank you for the gift of what you tell us. If you bring the gun, the people will know that you are the supreme hero of Segu." Bakaridjan repeated, "In fourteen days I will go to Dosoke Zan. He may give me the gun of his own will or I shall kill him and take it from him." When Aminata, the Fula woman, heard this, she gave more gold to the two djeli, saying, "Yes, Bakaridjan will bring you the gun, for he is a man of great valor. He is the hero of my choice."

The djeli then approached Madiniko. They sang a praise song to him. They started to speak, but he answered sharply, saying, "Do not talk to me. You come into the house. You see I am here, but you address Bakaridjan first as if his bravery and accomplishments exceed those of all other men. You know I am Madiniko and you know what I have done in my life. You knew my father and what he did in his life. You have heard of my grandfather and his epic deeds. Yet you go first to Bakaridjan. You say, 'Bakaridjan this' and 'Bakaridjan that' as if no other hero amounted to anything. Why should I talk to you? You have insulted me, and if you were not the king's djeli I would punish you."

The djeli answered softly. They said, "Madiniko, do not be angry. There are three men here, all of them renowned for their momentous achievements. Yet the people of Segu have been talking about how the three of you gather in Aminata's house as if none of you claims precedence over the others. They ask, 'Where is the honor of heroes?' So we came to speak to all of you. If we spoke to Bakaridjan first, it does not mean we judge him to be greater than you or Bamana Diase. A son comes after his father, but that does not mean that the father was more noble or had more valor. We came here only because all Segu needs to know what has not yet been resolved, that is to say, which of you is the paramount hero."

Madiniko replied, "I hear you. I am still offended. But I listened to what you told Bakaridjan and you do not need to say it again. You want the gun of Dosoke Zan. He has great mystic powers given to him by the chief of jinns. Bakaridjan will never be able to defeat him. It is I, Madiniko, who will kill Dosoke Zan. I am the one who will bring the gun. After that you will have to sing my praise song before all others." The djeli said, "Yes, Madiniko, we hear you. We thank you for the gift of your words. Bring us Dosoke Zan's gun and we will know who is the greatest hero in Segu." The Fula woman, Aminata, said to the djeli, "Aaaah, yes. Here is more gold. Madiniko will bring you the gun. I am sure of it. I choose him above the others."

Then the two djeli went to where Bamana Diase was lying on his mat. They sang him a praise song. He said, "You come to me last, as if I were a small boy who does not know the meaning of things. There is no hero greater than I in all Segu. Why should I respect you? Why should I speak to you? Perhaps I should beat you with my garan. Though you are esteemed djeli you are uninformed about my deeds and those of my father and my grandfather. Those who understand the word *valor* think of my name first. Those who understand the power of weapons think of my weapons first. Though you are the king's djeli you have something to learn. Do not repeat to me what you told Bakaridjan and Madiniko. I heard it all. If you truly want the gun of Dosoke Zan, do not be concerned about it. In fourteen days I will place it in your hands." The djeli answered, "Thank you, Bamana Diase, for what you have promised." And Aminata gave the djeli more gold, saying, "Yes, what Bamana Diase says is true. He is the one who will give you the gun. He is surely the most valorous."

After the two djeli departed from Aminata's house, the three heroes went to their homes. Now, even though they had spoken with assurance, Bakaridjan, Madiniko and Bamana Diase were not happy about what they had promised to do. They were restless and could not sleep. In the middle of the night each of them arose and went to consult his favorite morike.

Bakaridjan went to the morike named Serible Karamoko and told him of the challenge. Serible Karamoko said, "Aaaah, Bakaridjan, what you promised to do is impossible. There is no way for you to conquer Dosoke Zan. He is invulnerable to weapons and you cannot kill him because he is protected by the jinns. All I can do for you is to prevent you from being harmed." Bakaridjan replied, "Very well. Do what you can so that I may return safely from the fighting." Serible Karamoko went into another room and performed his mystic work. When he came back he gave Bakaridjan three white kola nuts, saying, "With these kolas you will make a saraka," meaning an act of charity. He said, "Give the kolas to a young boy with a light complexion. This will complete my work." Bakaridjan thanked the morike and went home.

Madiniko went to see a morike by the name of Drissa. When the morike heard Madiniko's story he said, "Aaaah! What you are planning to do is unfortunate, Madiniko. Dosoke Zan is under the protection of the jinns. You cannot kill him. Do not make the challenge. Let the other heroes try. But if you insist on going, perhaps I can do something to protect you from harm." Madiniko said, "Yes, do what you can." So Drissa went to another room and did his mystic work. He returned. He handed Madiniko three red kola nuts, saying, "Tomorrow morning perform a saraka with these kolas. You must give them to a young boy with a dark complexion. After that I can do no more for you." Madiniko said, "Thank you." He returned to his house.

The third hero, Bamana Diase, went to a morike named Kalifa and told his story. Kalifa said, "Bamana Diase, what have you done? You made a foolish promise. Don't you know that Dosoke Zan is protected by the jinns? No tafo made by a morike can overcome him. All I can do for you is to keep you alive." Bamana Diase said, "To be alive is good. Give me something to keep me alive." The morike said, "Tomorrow morning perform a saraka by giving a portion of goat meat to a young boy of black complexion. Cook the meat and have the boy eat it in your presence." Bamana Diase said, "I will do it." He returned to his home and slept.

But what is known to men is known to the jinns. The jinns overheard everything and reported to their chief, who went directly to the house of the hunter, Dosoke Zan. The chief jinn said, "Wake up. Bakaridjan, Madiniko and Bamana Diase are coming to challenge you and take your gun for a gift to the king's djeli. Go to the city early in the morning. Before entering the gate, sprinkle this powder on your body. It will make you resemble a young light-skinned boy. Then pass by the house of Bakaridjan Kone. He will give you a saraka of white kola nuts. After that, use the powder again and it will make you appear as a dark-skinned boy. Pass by the house of Madiniko and he will give you three red kolas. When you leave there, use the powder again. It will give you the appearance of a black-skinned boy. Go to the house of Bamana Diase, and he will give you a saraka of meat. Eat it, and when that is done return to your village."

Dosoke Zan did as the jinn instructed. He journeyed to the city in the darkness, arriving at sunrise. He sprinked the powder on his body and instantly took on the form of a young light-skinned boy. He walked along the street that led to Bakaridjan's house. When Bakaridjan saw him, he called out, "Boy, come here. I have something for you." Dosoke Zan approached Bakaridjan and waited. Bakaridjan took out the white kolas, put them in the palm of his hand and raised them toward the sky, reciting the saraka invocation:

> *You, Owner of the Water,*
> *You, Owner of the Land,*
> *You, Owner of All Humans,*
> *Witness my saraka.*
> *The Master of Diviners*
> *Said I should give a horse,*
> *But the horse is too big;*
> *That I should give a cow,*
> *But the cow is too big;*
> *That I should give a donkey,*
> *But the donkey is too big.*
> *Therefore I give these kolas as a saraka.*
> *I call on the Komo fetish,*
> *I call on the jinns,*
> *I call on the spirts of the dead:*
> *Protect me in my fight with Dosoke Zan.*
> *Nine eagles have performed their sarakas,*
> *Accept mine as the tenth.*

Nine hyenas have performed their sarakas,
Accept mine as the tenth.
If I have performed this saraka well,
May the Komo fetish, the jinns and the
  spirits of the dead accept it.

When the invocation was completed, Bakaridjan gave the three white kola nuts to the light-skinned boy, who was Dosoke Zan in another form, and went back into his house.

Dosoke Zan went to a hidden place, sprinkled powder on himself again and took on the form of a young dark-skinned boy. After this he walked past the house of Madiniko, who called out to him, "Éééé, boy, come here for a moment. I have something for you." Dosoke Zan approached. Madiniko held his three red kolas to the sky and recited the invocation to the Komo fetish, the jinns, and the spirits of the dead, after which he gave the kolas to the boy and reentered his house.

Again Dosoke Zan went to a hidden place and sprinkled the jinn's powder on himself. Instantly he became a boy of black complexion. He went then to the house of Bamana Diase, who called him to come and receive a saraka of goat meat. Bamana Diase recited the invocation and cooked the meat, which the boy ate. Dosoke Zan left the city and returned to his village, now, once more, in his real form.

The chief jinn came to him, saying, "Dosoke Zan, the three great heroes of Segu have delivered their magic powers into your hands by giving you their sarakas. Still, there are things that are not yet known. Every fighter goes into battle armed with mystic strength. But the greatest of all weapons is knowledge. There is something else to be done. Tomorrow morning take three eggs into the bush and place them next to a termite hill. The following day go and see if anything has happened to them. Each egg will represent one of your challengers. If the shell of any egg is damaged it will mean that one of the three heroes has the power to defeat you. In that case, unless you are willing to die, avoid the conflict."

Dosoke Zan followed the instructions of the jinn. He took three eggs into the bush and placed them next to a termite hill. The next day he went back to the termite hill and saw that the shell of one egg had been broken. He thought, "Aaaah! So one of them has the power

133

to kill me! It is decided. The chief jinn said that the greatest weapon is knowledge. Now knowledge speaks to me, saying, 'Decline to fight.' Or it says, 'Fight and die.' Knowledge gives me nothing to help me. Knowledge is a torment. Who can go out to fight knowing that his life is coming to an end? Yet who can turn away from the fight knowing that his honor and the honor of his family will be destroyed forever? I cannot do what the chief of jinns says. Perhaps the broken egg has no meaning at all. Whatever happens, I cannot refuse the challenge. Every hero has his time and somewhere it reaches its end. I will meet the heroes when they come."

When fourteen days had passed, Bakaridjan, Madiniko, and Bamana Diase rode together to the village where the hunter was living. They halted at the edge of the bush and waited. Soon they heard Dosoke Zan calling from a nearby place, saying, "You arrogant boys, why are you sitting there on your horses as if you were men of valor? Go into the village and join the children playing games. If you wish to fight, then fight. If you wish to sit, then go and sit with the women in the marketplace."

The three heroes said to one another, "Who will go first?" And Bakaridjan said, "I, Bakaridjan Kone, will go first." And he went forward and found Dosoke Zan astride his horse, his gun on his back, his cutlass across his chest and his spear in his hand. He said, "Dosoke Zan, you are known throughout Segu for your ability and your honor. But today is your last day. Let us fight. I will defeat you and take your gun to the djeli of the king." Dosoke Zan answered, "Yes, I know you, Bakaridjan Kone, and I know why you are here." Bakaridjan said, "I have not announced myself. How do you know my name?" Dosoke Zan said, "We have met before." Bakaridjan replied, "No, we have never met." Dosoke Zan said, "You are wrong. Don't you recall that you made a saraka in front of your house and gave three white kolas to a boy with a light skin? My friend, I was that boy. When you gave the saraka gift to me you placed all your magical strength in my possession. You have no chance to win. Your talismans are worthless. The mystic power given to you by your morike now belongs to me."

When Bakaridjan heard this he knew that he could not defeat Dosoke Zan. He knew that if he fought he would die. He said, "Dosoke Zan, I did not understand how it would be. I did not know that your magic was so powerful." Dosoke Zan replied, "Yes, I am protected by the chief of jinns. I am a Bambara and a noble. Because you are uncertain, I will not press the fight. You are free to turn and go back." Bakaridjan thought, "Aaah! How can I do it? I also am a Bambara and a noble. Never in the fiercest battle have I ridden away from the fighting. I have fought against armies, cities and kingdoms, but Dosoke Zan is more than an army, a city or a kingdom." He said aloud, "Dosoke Zan, I can see that it is hopeless. Do not despise me. I will not fight you. What I will face when I return home will be worse than dying. But I am drained of my strength. I will leave now and give the other heroes their chance." He turned his horse and rode away, knowing that in all Segu his prestige was gone.

Madiniko came next, riding to where Dosoke Zan was waiting. Dosoke Zan said, "Welcome, Madiniko. I was expecting you." Madiniko said, "I have not announced my name. How do you know it?" And Dosoke Zan told him what he had told Bakaridjan, saying, "When you made your saraka, it was to me that you gave the three red kolas. You placed all your magical protections in my hands. Now you are helpless." Madiniko said, "Aaaah!" His thoughts were the same as Bakaridjan's. At last he said, "Dosoke Zan, I cannot fight you." He rode away.

Then Bamana Diase came. Dosoke Zan said, "Welcome, Bamana Diase. I have been waiting for you. Do you remember me? I was the black-skinned boy to whom you gave your saraka." Bamana Diase replied, "Aaaah, was it you?" Dosoke Zan said, "I know everything about you and why you are here. Your magic is tied. Therefore ride away and save yourself." But Bamana Diase answered, "No, my friend, you are making a mistake. Today is your last day. No matter how great a hero may be, his time comes. Have you forgotten the broken egg?"

Dosoke Zan said, "An egg is fragile, it breaks easily. But how do you know of this matter?" Bamana Diase said, "I too have mystic powers. I know that the chief of jinns instructed you to place three eggs in the bush by a termite hill. I know he warned you that if one of the shells was broken you would be defeated. Through my mystic powers I came in the night and entered one of the eggs. I slept there. I awoke, I broke the shell of the egg and returned home. I am the man you cannot kill. Therefore, give me your gun and I will take it

135

back to the king's djeli." Dosoke Zan answered, "Aaaah! Then it was you. Yes, the chief jinn said, 'If one egg is broken it will announce your defeat, and so you should not accept the challenge.' But I am a freeborn Bambara. Because of my courage and my honor I am called a hero. I have never been defeated. If I now back away from you because of a broken egg, the people of Segu will laugh, ha, ha, ha, whenever I pass. They will say, 'There goes Dosoke Zan, who was once a hero but now he is nothing.'"

Dosoke Zan continued, saying, "You, Bamana Diase, think again. Despite the ill omen of the egg, I am prepared to fight you. If I die, I die. But I do not wish to die, and therefore I will fight with desperate effort. He who goes into battle accepting death is the most dangerous adversary. Perhaps the egg was wrong. Perhaps your morike was wrong. It is a new game. So withdraw your challenge, go away and live." Bamana Diase answered, "No, Dosoke Zan, it cannot be that way. I must fight for my honor and the honor of my family. Let us begin."

Bamana Diase said, "I give you the first chance." He rode his horse some distance away. Dosoke Zan dismounted, loaded his gun and kneeled on the ground. Bamana Diase came riding toward him. Dosoke Zan fired. The bullet struck Bamana Diase with great force and knocked him from his horse, but it did not penetrate his body. Bamana Diase stood up. He said, "You see, Dosoke Zan, I have mystic protections. You may try twice more." He rode back to his starting place and again came riding toward Dosoke Zan. Again the hunter fired his gun. And once again the force of the bullet knocked Bamana Diase from his horse without, however, harming him in any way. Bamana Diase said, "You see, my friend, it is hopeless. You have one more chance. This time your powder will not even catch fire." He returned to his starting place, and this time he came riding at great speed. Dosoke Zan thought, "When he falls from his horse I will kill him with my cutlass before he gets up from the ground." He pulled the trigger of his gun, but the spark did not ignite the powder and the bullet remained in the barrel. Bamana Diase did not stop. He rode his horse directly at the hunter and trampled him.

Dosoke Zan lay stunned and injured. Bamana Diase dismounted and took him by the hair, saying, "Dosoke Zan, it is over. Or do you want to continue the battle?" Dosoke Zan answered, "No, I have no more strength. Take my head and let it be finished." Bamana Diase said, "I do not want your head, Dosoke Zan, but I will take you and your gun to Segu for the king's djeli."

He returned to the city with his captive and brought him to the king's djeli. He gave them the gun, saying, "Here is what I promised you. Now it will be clear to everyone that I, Bamana Diase, am the paramount hero of Segu." The djeli replied, "Yes, the question is resolved. You, Bamana Diase, are the greatest of our heroes." They sang a praise song in his honor, but they would not accept Dosoke Zan as a slave. They said, "Dosoke Zan is a Bambara noble. He has achieved great deeds in his time. Let him go back to his village as a free man." So Dosoke Zan was freed and allowed to return to his village, but as he had been defeated, and in particular because he had not fought to the death, his prestige was much diminished.

As for Bakaridjan Kone, he was no longer esteemed because he had turned away from combat with Dosoke Zan. Whenever his name was mentioned, people laughed. When he walked through the streets, children chased him, calling, "Bakaridjan, where is the gun?" Or they shouted, "Bakaridjan, Bakaridjan, Bakaridjan" in time with his footsteps. He no longer met to talk and drink with the other heroes of Segu. He hardly left his house because of his shame, and after a while he did not come out at all. Many times he thought, "I should have fought and died. Then the djeli would now be singing my praise songs." He was no longer seen in public, and the city began to forget him.

After many months, on a certain festive holiday, the king's djeli said to one another, "Things are not the same without Bakaridjan Kone. It is true that he faltered, but he performed great deeds for Segu that cannot be forgotten. Let us go to his house and bring an end to his seclusion." The djeli took their ngonis and went to Bakaridjan's house and greeted him, saying, "You, Bakaridjan Kone, son of Mankoro, son of Kekeleka, son of Ngolo, we are here to remember your family and your accomplishments."

They sang praise songs to Bakaridjan, and afterward they asked him for the gift of a cow. He gave them a cow, but it was small and thin. The djeli said, "Aaaah, Bakaridjan, it is a poor cow you are offering us. We would rather have a fat cow from the city of Samaniana." This was before the destruction of Samaniana, and that city was still flourishing. It was said by many that no cattle anywhere could equal those of Samaniana. What the djeli asked of a noble he could not refuse, even a most extravagant gift. Now, one cow was not much, but when the djeli made their request they were thinking of a way for Bakaridjan to retrieve his honor. To give them what they asked for Bakaridjan would have to make an expedition against King Bassi's city. Bakaridjan replied, "Do not be concerned. I will bring you your cow. I will bring all of Samaniana's cattle, and not one shall remain behind. I will bring cattle for you, your wives, the blacksmiths of Segu, the leatherworkers of Segu and all the other people of Segu." The djeli said, "Aaaah, that is good."

A certain tonjon lurking outside Bakaridjan's house overheard the conversation. Hoping to gain a reward, he hurried to Samaniana and informed the king of what Bakaridjan proposed to do. Samaniana Bassi thanked the tonjon and gave him the gift of a cow. The tonjon took his cow to the marketplace and sold it for cowries, and with the cowries he bought cloth, after which he returned to the city of Segu.

Bakaridjan prepared himself for his expedition, and in a few days he began the journey, accompanied by his son, Simbalan Kone; his personal slave, Tchenbleni; and also by a party of twenty-nine Fulabafli, that is to say twenty-nine free Fula warriors. When Bakaridjan and his men approached Samaniana, King Bassi did not send his army out to meet them. Instead, he ordered that all the city's cattle be brought inside the walls, and when that was done the gates were closed and barred.

There was a young hero in Samaniana who did not like what the king had done. He thought, "Why does Samaniana Bassi hide in a dark corner because of the sight of Bakaridjan Kone?" He went to the king and said, "Great Bassi, you are the owner of the city, the walls, the crops, the cowries, the gold, the cattle and the wine of Samaniana. Whatever you say, I cannot contradict it, and whatever you say, I cannot countermand it. But who, after all, is Bakaridjan that we should bring in our cattle and bar our gates? He is a man. Why should we increase his reputation by refusing to fight with him? You are king of Samaniana, but I am king of myself. I am a freeborn person. My gun and my cutlass do what I tell them to do. I do not wish to remain indolent here in the city while Bakaridjan camps with his little army outside. Therefore I am going out to challenge him."

Samaniana Bassi answered, "Yes, my son, you are the king of yourself and the master of your own life. But victories are won not only by valor, but by discretion and intelligence. You underestimate Bakaridjan. I give you a proverb: 'Although the calf does not know the strength of the lion, the mother cow knows it.' No one can stop Bakaridjan. He has conquered more than twenty cities. There is no need to fight with him. Within the city we have bulging granaries and ample grazing for the cattle. Let us allow Bakaridjan to sit outside the walls until he is tired, then he will return home."

But the young hero said, "No, it would be dishonor for me if I did not go out to fight with Bakaridjan." He armed himself, put on his talismans, mounted his horse and went out of the city, but before he ever reached the place where Bakaridjan was camped, he was surrounded by warriors of the Fulabafli and killed. On hearing the news, Samaniana Bassi said, "The calf did not understand the strength of the lion. Now, these are my words: The gates will remain closed and no one else will go out of the city."

Bakaridjan remained outside the walls for forty days without finding a way to pass through the fortifications of Samaniana. He had no choice but to return to Segu. Because he was ashamed that he had not accomplished his objective, he and his men entered Segu secretly in the middle of the night and made their way unseen to their houses. Bakaridjan himself stayed in his house with his family and servants, never showing himself in the streets. If someone came to his door asking for him, his slave would say, "No, Bakaridjan is not here. He is on an expedition."

Bakaridjan's son, Simbalan Kone, aspired to be a great hero, even surpassing his father. He wanted to do one thing and another to prove his valor, but Bakaridjan would tell him, "My son, it is not yet time for you to perform great deeds. Your place is here with me. Be patient. Meanwhile, I am going to give you an important task. I do not want it to be known that I am living here in my house. If someone comes in or goes out at night when the city is sleeping, the secret may be revealed. Therefore, your task is to guard the outer entrance from nightfall to daybreak. Lie on the roof of the outer bulo with your gun. Let no one enter or depart." Simbalan Kone answered, "Yes, my father, I will do it." And every night he climbed to the roof of the outer bulo with his gun and guarded the entrance.

Each morning after sunrise, Simbalan went to his father's private quarters and greeted him, saying, "Good morning, my father." And Bakaridjan, pleased with his son, answered with a good-humored jest, saying, "My son, marahaba," marahaba meaning "son of a bad woman." And Simbalan replied to the joking insult by saying "Aaaah, my father, it is said that great heroes die young, but you have lived a long time. How can it be explained? I come and say, 'Good morning, my father,' but it will never be the same with me. I will not have a son to greet me this way, for I will be too occupied with heroic actions to marry and have a family." Though they spoke this way in good humor, Simbalan Kone genuinely had the intention of acquiring greatness beyond that of Bakaridjan.

After much time had passed, the djeli of the king began to wonder about Bakaridjan. They went from place to place, asking "Have you heard anything about Bakaridjan Kone who went on an expedition to Samaniana? Do you know where he is? Do you know what happened?" People answered, "No, we have not heard anything." If the djeli asked a member of Bakaridjan's household the answer was the same.

One day Bakaridjan's personal slave, Tchenbleni, came to him and said, "Master, I have a plan to outwit Samaniana Bassi. I will go to him and say that you are no longer living. Then he will open the gates of the city and send the cattle out. The rest will be up to you." Bakaridjan replied, "Aaaah, Tchenbleni, this is a good plan. When the cattle come out I will be waiting to challenge Bassi and his warriors to fight. I will retrieve my honor and prestige."

Tchenbleni said, "My master, there is one difficulty. I must leave in the dark of night to keep the secret. But Simbalan guards the gateway and will kill anyone who tries to pass." Bakaridjan said, "He is conscientious. He wants to perform a deed of valor. He is impatient for success and honor. He wants to excel me. Therefore, tell him that you can get a mystic talisman from the bush that will make him more heroic than his father. Then he will let you pass."

That night Tchenbleni tried to pass through the gateway, but Simbalan called out from the roof of the bulo, "Stop or I will shoot."

The slave said, "It is I, Tchenbleni." Simbalan answered roughly, "Who you are makes no difference. I would tell the king the same. No one passes through here." The slave said, "Morria! You are nothing! Who are you to speak this way? You are not a hero, only a child playing with a gun that is too big for you. You are not equal to your father. Without the help of mystic science you can never be equal to your father. So do not make your mouth so big." Although Tchenbleni was only a slave, he was Bakaridjan's age, and therefore Simbalan had to give him respect. Simbalan remained silent.

Tchenbleni said, "Now that we agree that you are only an ambitious boy and not a hero, I will tell you something. I can help you. At a certain place in the bush there is a tree from which special medicine can be made. That is where I was going when you stopped me. Because I know your mother's family well, I have a good feeling for you. Tonight I could not sleep, thinking, 'Simbalan wants to surpass his father's valor, but he cannot do it without medicine made from a secret tree in the bush. I will go in the darkness, so that Bakaridjan will not know, and get leaves from the secret tree. I will make medicine and apply it to Simbalan's body, so that he will have the mystic strength to perform spectacular deeds.' Therefore I arose from my sleeping mat and tried to go into the bush, but a stupid boy on the roof of the bulo threatened to kill me with his gun. So now I will go back to my mat and sleep."

Simbalan said, "Éééé, my father, you do not understand. Bakaridjan instructed me to do what I did. I obeyed him like a faithful son. I had no way of knowing what you were doing. You are an old and trusted member of the household. Do not hesitate. Go where you were going."

So Tchenbleni went out and departed from Segu. He journeyed for four days. When he arrived at Samaniana he was permitted to enter and he went directly to the king's house. It was clear from the way he dressed and wore his hair that he was a slave, but Samaniana Bassi was in his outer bulo and when he saw Tchenbleni he greeted him with courtesy. He asked, "Aaaah, slave, where are you from?" Tchenbleni answered, "Great king, I have just arrived from Segu." Samaniana Bassi asked, "Is my friend Da Monzon well?" Tchenbleni answered, "Yes, the king of Segu is well." After they conversed a while, Tchenbleni asked, "Great king, when I approached your city

I was perplexed, for I saw no cattle grazing, no farmers in the fields and no open gates. I wondered if Samaniana was alive and breathing."

Samaniana Bassi answered, "Aaaah, slave, Bakaridjan Kone came here to make trouble for us. I did not want to see men slaughtered in battle, so we brought in our cattle and closed the gates." Tchenbleni began to laugh. "Bakaridjan, did you say? You are protecting the city from Bakaridjan Kone? Great king, forgive me for laughing in your presence. I laughed only because here you are locked up in your city even though Bakaridjan is no longer among the living." Bassi exclaimed, "Éééé! You say Bakaridjan is dead?" The slave said, "Yes, after he came here to disturb you he returned to Segu. When he arrived there he found that Fula raiders from Massina had come and stolen all of Segu's cattle. So he made an expedition in pursuit of the Fula raiders and he was never again seen in Segu."

Samaniana Bassi said, "Aaaah! So he is dead. A fire may seem to breathe after its embers are cold. We thought he was out there in the bush. Slave, you have done a good thing to tell me about Bakaridjan. What is your name?" Tchenbleni answered, "Great king, my name is Mateh Minkorodon." In the Bambara language the name meant "what you cannot guess." The king said, "It is a strange name. To what family do you belong?" Tchenbleni answered, "I belong to the family called Abinaie." In Bambara the name meant "you will discover it," and Tchenbleni meant to imply that in time the truth would be revealed. The king gave Tchenbleni a cow to reward him. Tchenbleni took the cow, and in the market he exchanged it for cowries, and with the cowries he bought cloth and returned home to report to Bakaridjan. Bakaridjan prepared a new expedition, and in the darkness of the fourth night he left Segu once more, accompanied by his son, his slave and his twenty-nine Fula warriors. When they came within sight of Samaniana they encamped in a part of the bush where they would not be visible.

Samaniana Bassi reflected for several days on what he had heard about Bakaridjan's death, and at last concluded that there was no reason to be concerned about him. He ordered that the gates be opened and the cattle driven out to pasture. The king had a Fula slave named Fama who wanted to prove his valor. He went to Bassi and requested that he alone should take the cattle out of the city.

Samaniana Bassi said, "There are too many cattle for one man to watch. Who knows what dangers they might encounter out there?" Fama answered, "Great king, I have served your family all my life. I am a slave now, but my ancestors were freeborn men. Give me a gun. Grant me permission to take responsibility for all the cows of Samaniana." So Bassi ordered that a gun be given to Fama, and the slave drove the cattle out to graze in the bush.

Before traveling far he met Bakaridjan sitting on his horse. Bakaridjan said, "Slave, where are you going with the cattle?" Fama answered, "Cattle are grass eaters. I take them to the grass." Bakaridjan said, "These are the cattle of King Bassi and all his noble families. Where are the warriors who will protect them?" Fama replied, "I myself am the protector of the cows, as you can see." Bakaridjan said, "I am Bakaridjan Kone of Segu. I have come to take the cattle. So leave them with me now and go back to tell the king I am waiting to meet him and his heroes." Fama answered, "Aaaah, so you are Bakaridjan? They said Bakaridjan was dead." Bakaridjan said, "If what they said is true, then you are talking to a dead man on a horse. Go back and tell the heroes of Samaniana to come out and defend their honor." The slave said, "No, I will not do it. I am in charge of the cattle. Do you think a slave has no valor? Honor is not the exclusive property of nobles. I have my weapon. If you want to take the cattle you will have to fight for them."

Bakaridjan said, "Aaaah, slave, you are making things difficult. I cannot fight with a slave. What would the people of Segu say? They would say that I merely stole the cattle of Samaniana. I beg you, go back and tell the king that Bakaridjan Kone is waiting for Samaniana's valorous men to come out and defend what is theirs." The slave said, "You, Bakaridjan, you have no perception. I am here. If you want the cattle you must fight me for them. If you do not want them, go away and let me do my work." Bakaridjan argued, "I cannot fight a slave. I would be disgraced in all of Segu." The slave answered, "I am Fama, protector of the cattle. So fight or go away, whatever you choose."

Bakaridjan said at last, "Very well. I will have to kill you. Then perhaps Samaniana's heroes will appear." He dismounted. He allowed Fama to shoot at him three times, but the bullets did not penetrate his body. He said once more, "Fama, go now and tell

Samaniana Bassi that I am here." Fama did not listen. Using his gun as a club, he rushed forward and struck Bakaridjan with it. Bakaridjan said, "Aaaah, slave, this is more than I can allow. A slave may not strike a noble. Now I must kill you." He drew his cutlass from the scabbard across his chest. Just at that moment, Simbalan Kone raised his gun and shot Fama dead.

Bakaridjan turned and cried out, "Marahaba! Son of a bad woman! What do you think you are doing? Are you trying to proclaim yourself a hero over your father? You are valorous with your gun against a disarmed slave. I would have beaten him with the flat of my cutlass and preserved my honor. You wish to be greater than your father. Marahaba!" In his anger, Bakaridjan began to pursue Simbalan through the bush. Because of his youth, Simbalan was fleet, but Bakaridjan had the endurance of a tested hero. Bakaridjan caught Simbalan and threw him to the ground. He raised his spear, but Simbalan called out, "My father, stop. I want to quote a proverb before you kill me. We have been told, 'If you kill your bad dog, someone's good dog will bite you some day." Bakaridjan put down his spear. He did not kill Simbalan, even though the boy had thrown a shadow on his honor.

Bakaridjan returned to where the dead slave lay. He arranged the body so that the head pointed to the east and the feet to the west, and then he disemboweled it. He took his company of warriors to a hiding place not far away. In the city they heard the sound of the slave's gun, and the king's soldiers came out. They found Fama's body, and noting how it was arranged, some of the soldiers said, "See how it lies, pointing east and west, and disemboweled. That is the style of Bakaridjan." Others said, "No, King Bassi proclaimed that Bakaridjan no longer lives." Bakaridjan and his men came riding, their guns and spears in their hands, shouting out battle cries. King Bassi's heroes called to one another, "Bakaridjan Kone lives!" They fled back to the city. As it was said, "The bush became too small for them," meaning that they ran into one another in their panic and confusion. Bakaridjan pursued them and cut them down. When it was finished, numerous heroes of Samaniana lay dead on the earth. Others were captured and proclaimed to be slaves. Bakaridjan's Fula warriors rounded up the riderless horses and drove them, along with the cattle, back to the city of Segu.

From the housetops of the city the people of Segu saw an

enormous cloud of dust in the air. They said, "It seems as if an immense herd of cattle is approaching." And after a while they saw Bakaridjan Kone riding in the lead. They raised a shout, "Bakaridjan is returning! He who went to Samaniana and then disappeared has become visible again." Bakaridjan entered Segu. Numerous djeli sang praise songs to him. The city celebrated. Crowds filled the streets. And that night Bakaridjan and all the other heroes of Segu feasted and drank together.

The next morning Bakaridjan sent for the djeli who had launched him on his expedition to Samaniana. He spoke to them, saying, "You, great djeli of Segu, I gave you a small cow and you said, 'No, it is insignificant. What we want is a fat cow from Samaniana.' I said to you, 'I will bring back all of Samaniana's cows, and I will give you one and distribute the rest among your wives, the blacksmiths, the leatherworkers and all the other people of Segu.' It took me a long while, but finally I enticed Samaniana's heroes from behind their walls. There was a battle, and I cut them down like grass. I took horses, slaves and all the cattle of Samaniana. Choose your cow and I will distribute the rest as I promised. I will not keep a single cow for myself, only the slaves I captured." The djeli applauded Bakaridjan and sang new praise songs for him. Because of his successful expedition against Samaniana, Bakaridjan regained the respect of Segu, and his prestige was higher than ever before.

Deed upon deed, honor upon honor, generosity upon generosity, Bakaridjan Kone lived on. His name was known beyond the farthest reaches of the kingdom of Segu. When there were no longer any cities to conquer, no enemies of Da Monzon to chastise, no expeditions to lead, still Bakaridjan rode out to demonstrate his valor. Sometimes he was seen in Sahel, sometimes in Sansibara, sometimes in Woroguda, sometimes in Kurusabana, riding a white horse covered with silver trappings, alone except for his favorite slave who rode behind him. Though he had become wealthy from the booty of wars and the gifts of kings, Bakaridjan valued honor and achievement above all wealth. He gave gold to his friends, cowries to the poor and land and cattle to slaves.

Bakaridjan did not want anything that he did not have. He did not

145

want authority or power to rule cities or kingdoms. He did not aspire to anything but valor and honor. But even after many years, Da Monzon could not get it from his mind that Bakaridjan would try to take Segu away from him, that the brilliant star in the night sky would obscure the moon itself. He believed that something would have to be done soon to remove Bakaridjan from the minds of men and the songs of the djeli. He instructed his counselors and his agents to watch Bakaridjan closely for any kind of flaw in his loyalty.

It happened one evening that Bakaridjan was feasting and drinking with some other heroes of Segu. When heroes drank together they told one another of their experiences in this place or that place, and as they drank more they boasted of their personal exploits. First one hero recounted a valorous act that he had performed, then another told of his own great deeds. For a long while Bakaridjan was silent, but suddenly he felt the need to say something about himself. He said, "If I stamp my foot down it will make a hole in the ground so large that all of the kingdom of Segu could fit into it. And if all of Segu were to fall into that hole I could lift it out with one of my fingers." The heroes exclaimed, "Aaah!" And Bakaridjan continued, "If I myself were to fall into that hole all of Segu could not pull me out." The heroes exclaimed, "Aaah!" By this boast Bakaridjan was saying that he was stronger than Segu, and that without him there would be no Segu. While it was customary for heroes to boast when they were drinking, Bakaridjan's boast was excessive because it did not in some way acknowledge that Da Monzon was paramount over all other people and that the king's greatness surpassed all other greatness. So when news of Bakaridjan's boast was brought to Da Monzon it added fuel to the fire burning within the king. Da Monzon said, "Now, at last, Bakaridjan has fallen into the hole he stamped with his foot, and all of Segu will not be able to pull him out."

By ignoring the greatness of the king, Bakaridjan had denied the existence of the king, and this was treason. Da Monzon began immediately to prepare for the killing of Bakaridjan. He conspired to have Bakaridjan visit him in his private quarters and to have him shot down by the royal guards as he departed. To reach the king's personal house it was necessary to pass through six connected bulos, or antechambers. Da Monzon planned to conceal armed guards in each of the bulos. When the eating and drinking were over, Bakaridjan would depart and enter the sixth bulo, where the hidden guards would shoot him. If Bakaridjan managed to reach the fifth bulo alive, the guards in that bulo would shoot him. If he managed to reach the next bulo he would be killed there. Not even a hero such as Bakaridjan would be able to pass through the six anterooms and remain alive.

There was a saying among the Bambara: "Do not relate a matter of importance to a woman. Her stomach is not a secret treasure box." But Da Monzon was so stirred by the plot he had contrived that he told his favorite wife in confidence. In the same spirit of confidence, the favorite wife told an elderly slave woman. It would have ended there, except that the slave woman had been treated generously by Bakaridjan's son, Simbalan. He had always spoken to her with respect, as if she were not a slave, and often he had given her gifts. And so the woman went to Simbalan Kone and told him what she had heard. Simbalan decided that he would not tell his father, but would deal with the conspiracy by himself.

On a certain evening Da Monzon invited Bakaridjan to eat and drink with him in his private quarters. He said, "Bakaridjan, we are old friends. Let us feast together in my personal house. We will forget the reminders of combat and war. Leave your weapons at home, and I also will put my weapons away. We will talk and enjoy ourselves, and I will tell you some of the secrets of my life." Bakaridjan said, "Yes, I will come, and I will not bring any weapons." He came to the palace and passed through the six bulos and entered the king's house. After he had gone through the anterooms, the king's guards came in and hid themselves there, forty in each room, each with a gun.

Bakaridjan and the king sat together, feasting and drinking wine. Da Monzon offered Bakaridjan more and more wine to make him drunk. Now, although he had promised to put his weapons away, Da Monzon had hidden his gun under a cloth near where he sat. When he thought the time was right he took out the gun and pointed at Bakaridjan, saying, "I know everything about you, Bakaridjan. I know you do not have any talisman to protect you from the magic of this gun. So now I want you to speak. It was told to me that you boasted, 'If I stamp my foot down it will make a hole in the ground so

large that all of the kingdom of Segu could fit into it. And if all of
Segu were to fall into that hole I could lift it out with one of my
fingers. And if I myself were to fall into that hole all of Segu could
not pull me out.' So, Bakaridjan, I am ready to hear you repeat these
words. As you are a noble, you cannot back away from it. If you
acknowledge to my face what you have said, I will kill you. It is I
who made you a hero by giving you good treatment. It is I who fed
you and gave you honors. The valor of my armies has given you a
great name. Therefore your boast that you are greater than all Segu
is evil. Because you live by honor, do not shrink from repeating your
boast. When I have heard it from your mouth you will die."

Bakaridjan had drunk much wine, and he was not in command of
his mind. He said only, "Aaah!" Because he could not bring himself
to lie, all he could have said was, "Yes, those were my words," but to
say so would end his life instantly. He groped for something to tell
Da Monzon. The king said to him, "Very well, Bakaridjan, if you
cannot say those words, let me hear you say, 'I, Bakaridjan, am no
longer a hero. I am no longer a noble. I am a bastard.'" To speak
such words would have disgraced Bakaridjan and dishonored his
family forever. He prepared himself to die.

But Simbalan, Bakaridjan's son, conceived a way to deal with the
ambush set for his father. With the help of the elderly slave woman,
he had found a back way into the king's compound and a secret
entrance into the king's house. At the moment when Bakaridjan was
preparing himself to die, Simbalan entered the king's personal room
and pointed his gun at Da Monzon. He said to Bakaridjan, "My
father, you are the greatest hero in Segu. Before your time there
were no heroes like you, and after your time there will be no more
heroes like you. It was you who made Da Monzon's empire what it
is. Do not hesitate to repeat the boast that you made to the heroes."

Already Bakaridjan had planned to say the words, even if he had to
die for them. So now he spoke, saying, "If I stamp my foot down it
will make a hole in the ground so large that all of the kingdom of
Segu could fit into it. And if all of Segu were to fall into that hole I
could lift it out with one of my fingers. And if I myself were to fall
into that hole all of Segu could not pull me out."

Da Monzon said to Simbalan Kone, "Éééé, my son! You do not
understand. Your father and I are just playing a game. We are

friends." Simbalan answered, "No, it is not that way. You want to kill him." Da Monzon said, "No, we were merely drinking wine, and what was said between us is of no importance. Let us forget everything. You two, now, go home to sleep. The evening is over." Da Monzon was thinking of the ambush that awaited Bakaridjan in the six bulos.

Simbalan continued to point his gun at Da Monzon. He said, "Yes we will leave now. But to show us proper hospitality you should lead us though the bulos and accompany us to the gate. Great king, lead and we will follow." Da Monzon had no choice. He went ahead and they came behind. As they entered the sixth bulo, where forty men were hiding in the darkness with their guns, he called out, "Guards, do not do what I told you to do." So the guards did not shoot. Da Monzon, Bakaridjan and Simbalan passed through safely. As they entered the fifth bulo, Da Monzon called out, "Guards, what I told you to do, do not do it." At the fourth bulo it was the same, then at the third, the second and the first. No gun was fired, and Bakaridjan and Simbalan passed safely through the king's outer gate.

Because of Simbalan, Da Monzon's plot against Bakaridjan failed. Bakaridjan lived on. As before, he sought valor and honor in one place and another. His name grew greater still. Although Da Monzon could not stop believing that Bakaridjan was a threat to his prestige and power, he never again conspired against Bakaridjan's life. For he saw that Simbalan Kone would also be a formidable hero who would have the courage to avenge his father's death.

In Praise of Malamini Sinsani

ALAMINI SINSANI WAS A RICH MAN living in Sinsani in Banta Sako. He was renowned for the generous gifts that he gave to musicians and djeli. He gave gold, he gave cowries, he gave cattle, he gave slaves, he gave lavishly of everything, and it was said that no one ever gave more of anything than Malamini Sinsani. It was said that if a djeli received a gift from Malamini and said thank you, Malamini gave him more. And if the djeli again said thank you, Malamini again gave him a gift. Malamini did not stop giving gold or cowries until the djeli stopped saying thank you. The djeli of Segu sang this song praising Malamini's generosity:

> *Malamini Sinsani treated us handsomely.*
> *Malamini Sinsani gave us generous gifts.*
> *The Soninke women of Banta Sako say*

151

That if they do not marry Malamini they will never be happy.
If they do not marry Malamini
They cannot go on living.
If unkind words are spoken of Malamini
It will go badly for you.
If Malamini, son of Salufo, hears such words
It will go badly for you.
If the son of my friend Salufo hears such words
It will go badly for you.

I have traveled everywhere.
I have traveled to the country of the king.
I have traveled to the country of the great people.
I have traveled to the north country of great kings.
I never saw anyone like Malamini in the north.
I never saw anyone like Malamini in the south.
I never saw anyone like Malamini in the east.
I never saw anyone like Malamini in the west.
The women of Banta Sako get excited
When they see Malamini Sinsani.
They get so excited that their beaded waistbands break.

If you want to know Banta Sako
You must pass the house of Malamini Sinsani.
If you want to know who is important in Banta Sako
You must pass the house of Malamini Sinsani.
The people of today like new things
But there is no continuity in innovation.
People want to get married in the new way,
But there is no continuity in that.

I have traveled everywhere.
I have traveled to the country of the king.
I have traveled to the country of the great people.
I have traveled to the north country of great kings.
I never saw anyone like Malamini in the north.
I never saw anyone like Malamini in the south.
I never saw anyone like Malamini in the east.
I never saw anyone like Malamini in the west.
The women of Banta Sako get excited

IN PRAISE OF MALAMINI SINSANI

When they see Malamini Sinsani.
They get so excited that their beaded waistbands break.

When you are born for something
Nothing can change your destiny.
When you are born to be rich
You will be rich and nothing can alter it.
Malamini is rich and generous,
Malamini Sinsani of Banta Sako.

In the town of Yemina also there was a very rich man, and his name too was Malamini. He was called Malamini Yemina. Like Malamini Sinsani he was very generous to djeli and musicians, and people began to dispute which of the two men gave the greater gifts. Malamini Yemina invited Malamini Sinsani to come to a festival at his village so it could be seen which of the two was more generous.

Malamini Sinsani arrived in Yemina. The festivities began in the afternoon, with many musicians and djeli assembled. The rich Malamini of Yemina gave cowries to the djeli. The rich Malamini of Sinsani gave cowries to the djeli. They gave cowries to the musicians. Darkness fell. The singing went on. Malamini Yemina gave gold to the djeli. Malamini Sinsani gave gold to the djeli. They gave out gifts of money all night, and when morning came no one could say who had given most generously. Malamini of Sinsani returned home.

The controversy over which Malamini deserved more praise for his generosity continued. Malamini Sinsani's chief djeli said to him, "The discussion still goes on. Nothing has been resolved. What has begun, let us continue it here in Sinsani." Malamini agreed. His djeli said, "The gift-giving contest should be held under the great tree in your courtyard. Give your son a bag of cowries and let him climb to the top of the tree. When you call out to him, let him rain the cowries down from above." Malamini Sinsani assented, and he sent an invitation to Malamini Yemina to come for a continuation of their gift-giving contest.

Malamini Yemina arrived. All the djeli and the musicians played. And when a djeli had sung a praise song, first one Malamini gave presents, then the other. They gave many cowries and much gold. All night long the gift giving went on. At last, when the light of

153

morning came, they had no more gifts to give. Malamini Yemina said, "We both have been generous with the djeli. We have given everything. How can it be said which of us earned the greatest merit?"

But Malamini Sinsani said, "Oh, no, I am ashamed not to have given more. I cannot stop now." He went and stood under the great tree. He raised his arms upward and called out, "Allah, help me. I am miserable. Because I have given so little to the djeli I will not be able to eat or sleep. I must be more generous, or what will people say of me? What will the djeli sing of me in their praise poems? Help me not to lose my merit and my good name."

When Malamini Sinsani spoke these words, his son in the top of the tree opened his bag and showered the cowries upon the heads of all those assembled below. Malamini Sinsani ordered that the cowries be gathered and given to the djeli. Malamini Yemina said, "Who is there in the world to compete with Malamini Sinsani? He has a treasury in the sky." He departed from Sinsani and returned to his house in Yemina. The djeli sang:

> *When you are born for something*
> *Nothing can change your destiny.*
> *When you are born to be rich*
> *You will be rich and nothing can alter it.*
> *Malamini is rich and generous*
> *Malamini Sinsani of Banta Sako.*

DIULADJAN DIABI, A SONINKE HERO OF KIBAN

THIS STORY IS ABOUT DIULADJAN DIABI, a hero of the city of Kiban in the time when Amadu was king of Segu. Kiban was one of the Seven Cities of the Maraka, or Soninke, people. Though the Soninke were not Bambara, and though they belonged to the world of Islam, still the cities were under the authority of the kings of Segu. When a djeli sang a praise song for the king, he might begin by saying, "You who are the lion of the bush, you who are the owner of the Four Segus and the Seven Marakas." Kiban was the leader of the Seven Cities. It was Kiban that collected taxes for the king. It was Kiban that spoke to the king for the others.

But Kiban was not always great. Before it emerged, there was only wild bush in that place, and the nearest settlement was a large Bambara town called Djekoro Bugu, whose chief was called by the

155

same name, Djekoro. The djeli tell us that Djekoro Bugu was two
miles in length. Chief Djekoro's house was at one end of the town
and his mother's house was at the other end. Each morning when
the chief arose he went outside and greeted his mother in this
manner: The people of Djekoro Bugu formed two lines extending
from the chief's house to his mother's house, three hundred persons
in each line. The chief said, "Good morning, my mother." The
nearest person in the first line turned to the second and said, "Good
morning, my mother." And the second turned to the third and said,
"Good morning, my mother." The third person relayed the greeting
to the fourth, and the fourth to the fifth, and the words traveled
along the column until they arrived at the mother's house. In
response, the chief's mother said, "Good morning, my son," and her
words would be relayed person to person along the second column
until they reached the ears of her son Djekoro. Thus we know
something of the extent of Djekoro Bugu. It was populous and rich,
and its chief owned many slaves and had good fighting men.

It happened one time that a large party of Soninke travelers, led by
a family named Diabi, arrived in the vicinity of Djekoro Bugu. They
went to the chief and asked permission to settle in his town. Djekoro
said, "You Maraka, are you not Muslim? And we Bambara, are we
not Bambara? No, we cannot take any Maraka people in Djekoro
Bugu. Our ways conflict with one another. There would be
dissension. Still, it appears that you have been on a long journey, so I
will give you some land out there in the bush and you can build your
houses and clear your fields. I also give you permission to hunt game.
Let no Maraka among you ever say that Djekoro is not generous."

The chief sent one of his counselors to show the Soninke where
they could build a village and plant their crops. The Soninke built
their village. They cleared their fields and planted. And because they
were devout Muslim people they built a mosque. They gave their
village the name Kiban. At prayer time a muezzin mounted to the
highest point of the mosque and gave his azan. When the people
heard the azan, they prayed to Allah. Though Kiban and Djekoro
Bugu were some distance apart, the muezzin's call nevertheless
could be heard in the Bambara town, which annoyed the chief. He
sent for the leaders of the Soninke and told them, "We are Bambara
here. Your muezzin's voice floats in the air all around us. I don't

want the word Allah heard in Djekoro Bugu. I forbid you to disrupt our town anymore with these calls."

The Soninke were on land given to them by Djekoro. They were weak and Djekoro Bugu was strong, so they could not defy the chief's command. But they were not willing to bring their religious practices to an end. What they did was to instruct the muezzin to call the azan very softly so that his voice would not carry across the bush to Djekoro Bugu. As time passed, other Soninke families arrived at Kiban. The village grew large. It became a town. Morikes came from other places and settled there, and Kiban had the aid of the mystic sciences. Traders found their way to Kiban from distant cities. And little by little, the hunters of Kiban developed into a force of resolute fighters. The morikes performed secret rituals that protected the fighters from spears and bullets, and the numukes who made the weapons forged them in a way to make them irresistible. It was taboo for a man of Kiban to look into the barrel of a gun, for if he did so he would become blind. So the warriors and hunters carried their guns on their backs, barrels pointing upward, and when a man had to load his gun he did so by reaching over his shoulder. Kiban became strong. And because more and more Soninke came there to have protection from the Bambara, the people went to Djekoro and asked him for more land. He gave it to them, and so Kiban expanded.

But Djekoro became fearful. The Soninke were spreading the beliefs of Islam. Chiefs of small villages became Muslims, ordinary people were becoming Muslims. Djekoro thought, "If these things go on we Bambara will become nothing but islands with the water of Islam surrounding us." He became repressive toward Kiban and other Soninke settlements. He harassed the Soninke. He made their lives difficult. He quarreled with them over their hunting, accusing them of killing game that belonged to Djekoro Bugu. He quarreled with them over their taxes, demanding more. In matters of justice, he was harsh with the Soninke at the same time that he was generous with the Bambara. He even threatened to destroy the mosque in Kiban.

At last the people of Kiban could no longer tolerate Djekoro. They sent an emissary to Djekoro to say, "Greetings to you, great chief, from the people of Kiban, the army of Kiban, the numukes of Kiban, the djeli of Kiban and the slaves of Kiban. We are the people to whom you gave land for our houses and our fields. When we first arrived we thought, 'Djekoro is a great man. Though he does not like to hear our muezzin chanting the azan, still he will treat us fairly.' Before Allah all people are equal, but you have not treated us as equals. You have treated us as a vassal city that you conquered. But Kiban of today is not the same Kiban whose muezzin you told to keep quiet. You cannot treat us harshly anymore. Therefore I have been told to ask you to renounce all authority over Kiban, to relinquish all our taxes, to take no more men from Kiban for your work projects and to accept us as absolute equals in every way. If you accept these conditions we will ask nothing more, but if you reject them then we will have to visit you and have a discussion with our weapons."

When Djekoro heard this message he told the emissary, "Go back to your collection of huts that you call Kiban. Tell your people that they are of the caste of slaves. They came here begging a little land, which I gave them. Then they begged a little more land, which I gave them. They prospered because I protected them from predators. Because your men can walk on two legs, that does not make them heroes. Every slave has two legs. Because they hunt, that does not make them heroes. Even a bush rat can hunt. Let us not waste any words. The Maraka know nothing but farming. They cannot fight. If your people decide to come, let them come with tight lips because there will be no conversation between us. Let them bring their own wine, for we will not send them any from inside the town. Let them bring their own jokes, because we will give them nothing to make them laugh."

The emissary returned to Kiban and reported everything. So Kiban prepared for war. Its morikes applied their mystic sciences to protect men's bodies and make bullets fly true. And when at last it was ready, Kiban's army took the road to Djekoro Bugu, and just as they came within sight of the walls Djekoro's fighters came out and took their positions. The battle began, and there was the sound of guns and steel beating on steel. Before nightfall Djekoro's fighters were defeated. The bards do not tell us whether the Soninke took Djekoro's head, but they say that Djekoro's people were driven away and the town destroyed. They say that the survivors of Djekoro Bugu migrated elsewhere and built new villages in a far-off place.

From that battle there emerged several Soninke heroes, and one of them was Diuladjan Diabi, a son of the highest-ranking family of Kiban. Still other heroes migrated to Kiban from various Soninke cities. Kiban's fame grew large. It is said that the greatest of Kiban's heroes were Diuladjan Diabi, Bakore Samassa and Madine Diabi, and that these men led expeditions against many other Bambara towns and defeated them. Diuladjan Diabi married, had children, land, cattle and more than a thousand slaves.

The djeli tell us that Diuladjan Diabi once went to war not to conquer a city, not to glorify the name of Kiban, not to expand the influence of Islam, but because his favorite wife decided she needed a certain kind of milk for her bassi, a food made of millet.

One day the favorite wife's personal slave came to Diuladjan and told him, "Your wife refuses to eat her bassi. We urged her. We cajoled her. But she said, 'Go away, I am finished with eating bassi.' Perhaps she is ill. Therefore I came to let you know." Diuladjan went to his favorite wife. He was concerned about her health. He said, "Why is it that you refuse to eat bassi? Is something wrong?" She replied, "My husband, it is because of the milk. I cannot eat bassi made with the milk of the cows of Kiban." Diuladjan said, "What is wrong with the milk of the cows of Kiban?" She answered, "I do not wish to have it." Diuladjan said, "I do not understand. Kiban has the finest of cows." His favorite wife said, "I will not eat bassi anymore unless I can put into it milk from the cows of Woro." Diuladjan said, "Unless you eat bassi you will grow weak and die." His wife said, "Yes, I am prepared, but I can be saved if I can have milk from the cows of Woro." Diuladjan said, "Be a little patient. It will take time. But I will bring cows for you from Woro." He remembered the saying, "The wish of a woman is the wish of Allah."

Woro was a Bambara town of courageous fighters, among whom were three brothers whose valor was often celebrated in the poems of the djeli. Diuladjan Diabi prepared himself to go to Woro. When the two other famous fighters of Kiban, Bakore Samassa and Madine

159

Diabi, heard what he was going to do they came to him and said, "We are going with you to Woro." But Diuladjan said, "No, my good friends, I must go alone. I am not going for fame and honor. I am going because my favorite wife has asked me to bring her cows from Woro. She did not ask Kiban to do it. She did not ask the nobles of Kiban to do it. She did not ask the slaves of Kiban to do it. She asked me, Diuladjan Diabi. Therefore I must do it alone." He took up his weapons and mounted his horse, with his personal slave as his only companion. He said to his favorite wife, "I am beginning the journey. But if I do not return within a week, make my black funeral cloth ready."

He made the journey to Woro. When he arrived at the outskirts of the town he went to where two Fula herdsmen were guarding the cows. He said to them, "I am taking the cattle to Kiban." They answered, "Do you know what you are saying? These cattle belong to the nobles of Woro." Diuladjan Diabi said, "Yes, that is why I have come for them. Open the gate of the cattle pen and drive them out." They answered, "Do you know what you are doing? We have great heroes here in Woro." Diuladjan Diabi said, "Yes, I know. But you are the Fula herdsmen. Therefore drive the cattle out." One of the herdsmen took up a position in front of Diuladjan Diabi, saying, "This town belongs to Bambara people. You are Maraka." Diuladjan Diabi said to him, "Herdsman, do what I say. I did not come to fight you." The herdsman raised his spear, whereupon Diuladjan drew his sword and killed him. The second herdsman opened the gate and drove out the cattle. Diuladjan instructed his slave to take the cows back to Kiban, and he told the herdsman to go and report to the chief what had happened. Then he spread his camel-hair blanket on the ground and lay down on it to rest.

The herdsman reported to the chief of Woro that a warrior from Kiban had seized the town's cattle. The chief went immediately to the father of the three hero brothers of Woro, saying, "Send your sons out at once to kill the pillager of our livestock." The father said, "Aaah! One will be enough to deal with him. I will send my oldest son." So the oldest son armed himself, mounted his horse and rode away. He found Diuladjan Diabi resting on his blanket. Diuladjan said, "You, Bambaraka, don't you see I am resting? Why do you disturb me?" The man replied, "Someone has come and stolen our cattle. I am looking for him." Diuladjan answered, "You do not have to look any further. I am Diuladjan Diabi of Kiban. I am the one who took the cows."

The Bambara hero said, "You, a Maraka, came alone to steal our herds? A farmer comes to challenge warriors of Woro? Think again. Return the cows. I will let you go. I do not want people to say I fought with a Maraka farmer." Diuladjan answered, "Turn and go back. Your mother and father are worried about you. They are saying, 'What is our son doing out there pretending to be a hero?' Go back quickly and let them know you are safe."

The Bambara hero said, "Your words are like little feathers floating in the air. They will not help you. Your resting time is finished. Stand up, we will fight." Diuladjan stood up. The fighting began. The Bambara said, "I will allow you to shoot first." Diuladjan said, "No, I am the one who took your cows. Therefore you should shoot first." The Bambara said, "You are right, Maraka. I am going to kill you now." He raised his gun and fired, but because Diuladjan had been treated by a morike, the bullet did not hurt him. Diuladjan said, "Try again." The Bambara fired again, but again the bullet failed to harm him. He tried a third time, but it was the same as before. Then the Bambara hero drew his cutlass and struck with it, but though the blade was keen it could not even make a mark on Diuladjan's skin. After that it was Diuladjan's turn. He drew his cutlass from its scabbard. The blade was not made of steel or brass, but of a mysterious metal that had come from a far-off place. The Bambara's protective medicine was useless, and Diuladjan killed him with a single stroke.

Now, when the eldest of the hero brothers did not return, the second came out of the town and challenged Diuladjan, and the outcome was the same. When the second did not return, the third came, and Diuladjan killed him as well. Diuladjan entered the town and went to the chief's house. He said to the chief, "I am Diuladjan Diabi of Kiban. I have taken all your cattle. I have been lying on my blanket waiting for a great hero to come and challenge me. What is the matter with Woro?" The chief answered, "Aaah! We sent three champions to challenge you. What happened?" Diuladjan said, "Yes, three inexperienced boys came. I killed them all. Where are Woro's heroes? Send another one to fight me." The chief answered, "No,

Diuladjan of Kiban, if you have killed the three brothers, let it rest there. We have no one better to give you."

Diuladjan returned to Kiban bringing with him the cows of Woro. He chose the finest of the cows and gave it to his favorite wife, saying, "Now you can be happy again. You have what you asked me to get for you." His wife said, "Yes. Now once more I can eat bassi."

In addition to the Seven Cities of the Soninke, scattered among them there also were other towns and villages of Muslim belief. One of these towns was called Niare, and its name was remembered for generations by the djeli who sang of the history of Kiban and the deeds of Diuladjan Diabi:

> *How can a person say "Niare"?*
> *To speak the word Niare is bitter.*
> *One hundred first-born heroes went from Kiban,*
> *And only the hero Diuladjan Diabi returned.*

In the town of Siribi there was a famous warrior by the name of Ntiyi, and he was known as Siribi Ntiyi. He was fierce and ruthless in war, and he looked for fame wherever he could find it. He came riding to the town of Niare one day with his personal djeli and a company of fighting men. He said to the chief and the notables of Niare, "I am looking for the Maraka hero Diuladjan Diabi." They were fearful of Ntiyi. They replied, "Diuladjan Diabi does not live here." Ntiyi said, "I do not care where he lives. He is Maraka. You are Maraka. Get him for me. I want him." They answered, "How can we do it? It is impossible." Ntiyi said, "Aaah! You people of Niare, do you want to live or to die? If you do not give Diuladjan Diabi to me I will destroy your town. Those of you who are fit to be slaves, I will take as slaves, and the rest I will leave to feed the hyenas and crows. I give you five days, and on the fifth day you must put Diuladjan Diabi in my hand." Siribi Ntiyi and his fighting men took up quarters in Niare and remained there.

The chief of Niare and his counselors debated what they could do to survive Siribi Ntiyi. They conspired to bring Diuladjan Diabi to Niare. They sent a message to Kiban saying that the Bambara of Siribi were going to attack Niare within five days. They pleaded for Diuladjan to come and help them defend the town. The counselors of Kiban decided to send one thousand fighters to protect Niare. But Diuladjan said, "No, one thousand is too many. Give me ninety-nine eldest sons of Kiban. I will lead them." The chief and the counselors agreed. Ninety-nine eldest sons of Kiban volunteered to go with Diuladjan. They prepared their weapons. They mounted their horses and departed.

When they arrived at Niare the day was giving way to night. The people came out and greeted the fighters from Kiban, saying, "Welcome. We are grateful that you are here to help us." They brought Diuladjan and his men inside the walls. They said, "Leave your weapons here in the chief's armory. The battle will not begin until tomorrow. Tonight we will eat, drink wine and dance." The men of Kiban stacked their weapons in the chief's armory. Diuladjan placed his gun there, but kept his cutlass, made of mystic metal, with him, because it was his habit to sleep with it at his side. There was feasting and dancing. And when the night grew late, Kiban's warriors were given ten houses in which to sleep, ten men to each house. They lay down and slept.

Then the people of Niare went to where Siribi Ntiyi and his fighters were hiding. They said, "You promised to spare Niare if we placed Diuladjan Diabi in your hands, and now we give him to you." They pointed out the ten houses where Diuladjan's fighters were sleeping, saying, "They have no weapons. They belong to you."

To save themselves the people of Niare had abandoned their honor. But they were not alone, because Ntiyi was a noble and he cast away the chivalrous code of noble heroes. He took his fighters and entered first one and then another of the houses where the unarmed men of Kiban slept, slaughtering them as they attempted to rise from their mats. Diuladjan, who slept with only one eye closed, heard sounds in the night. He took his cutlass and aroused the others in his house, saying, "Unbelievable things are happening. Niare has committed treachery against us. Save yourselves if you can." He went out and saw Siribi Ntiyi's warriors attacking the ten houses. He ran to where the horses were kept and found his own horse. He mounted and rode swiftly from the town. Outside the walls, a party of Ntiyi's men tried to stop him, but he cut his way through with his cutlass into the bush, the enemy following him. At a certain place he halted. When the first of the pursuers arrived, Diuladjan killed him. He took the man's gun and bullets, and with the gun and his cutlass he fought against the enemy. He killed many fighters from Siribi. He killed relentlessly, and the bodies of Ntiyi's men littered the ground. Diuladjan Diabi killed more than two hundred of the enemy, and when there were no more to fight, he rode back to Kiban in the darkness.

As the sun rose, the people of Kiban saw him coming. They were surprised to see him riding alone. They asked anxious questions. He said, "My brothers and sisters, he whom you see is alive. He whom you do not see is dead." So they understood that ninety-nine of their eldest sons had perished. The people said, "We have lost an entire generation in the treachery at Niare. It seems that our force is spent, and Kiban will never again be what it was."

Now, Tuba, one of the Seven Cities, had always envied Kiban because it was the king's representative among the Soninke. When it heard that a disaster had overtaken Kiban, it saw an opportunity to strengthen its position with the king of Segu. The chief of Tuba, along with a party of counselors, journeyed to the city of Segu and had an audience with King Amadu. They said, "Great king, Kiban is in disarray. Once it was strong, but it lost ninety-nine first-born sons in a battle at Niare, and now it is weak. It is no longer the sword and shield of the Seven Cities. We in Tuba are ready to take the responsibility. Whatever you tell us to do we will do. We will collect the taxes and deliver them to you. If you need fighting men for an expedition, we will see that the Seven Cities provide them." The king's counselors confirmed the disaster that had taken place at Niare. And finally Amadu said, "Yes, I appoint you. Henceforth Tuba will be my representative among the Seven Cities."

In time the news reached Kiban and caused great anger. The chief sent emissaries to Tuba. They asked, "Is it true that you went to Segu and asked that our authority be taken away from us? Is it true that the king appointed you his representative?" The chief of Tuba said, "Yes, it is true." The emissaries asked three times, and three times the chief of Tuba said, "Yes, it is true." They brought the word back to Kiban. Diuladjan Diabi said, "I myself will ask them." He went to the chief of Tuba and asked the question three times. The chief answered, "Yes, the king has appointed us to be his authority among the Seven Cities." Diuladjan Diabi said, "What the people of Niare did was treacherous. What you did also was treacherous. Niare maimed us and you rushed forward to lick the bones. I came here personally to let you know that Kiban is not dead. We have valorous men. Do you believe that Tuba is greater than Kiban? Very well, let us test each other."

Thereupon Diuladjan Diabi put forward a challenge. He said, "I speak now of two Bambara towns, Koniba and Tara. We will send an expedition against one, you will send an expedition against the other. In this way we will determine whether Kiban or Tuba has the most valor." The heroes of Tuba quickly answered, "Yes, we accept your challenge. But which of us goes against Tara and which goes against Koniba?" Diuladjan replied, "Choose one. We will take the other." The heroes of Tuba said, "We will go against Tara."

Tuba and Kiban both prepared themselves, and on a certain day they both went on their expeditions against the Bambara. The men of Tuba arrived at Tara, and the Bambara came out and fought with them. The struggle went on all day, and just before nightfall the Bambara won control of the battlefield and the fighters from Tuba were defeated. The heroes of Kiban arrived at Koniba, and the Bambara came out to meet them. There also the fighting was bitter, but the heroes of Kiban defeated the Bambara. In this way Diuladjan Diabi proved to Tuba that Kiban was still a city of valorous men.

Still, there were those in Tuba who said, "Yes, Kiban is valorous. But the army we fought at Tara was superior to the army Kiban fought at Koniba." When Diuladjan heard this he said, "How much proof does Tuba need that Kiban is a city of heroes? One man of Kiban can do what all of Tuba could not achieve." He went to an old morike and said to him, "I want you to prepare me. I am going alone to conquer Tara." The morike said, "To say 'conquer' is easy. Many men who said 'conquer' went out and never returned." But the old morike was wise in the mystic sciences, and he did his work. And while this was taking place, two of the other great heroes of Kiban,

Madine Diabi and Bakore Samassa, came to Diuladjan's house and said, "We are going with you." Diuladjan said, "Good," but he did not want them to come, because if he himself should not return, Kiban would need champions to protect it from the enemy. He said, "Wait for me tomorrow in Bakore Samassa's house. When I am ready I will come for you."

The next morning Diuladjan did not go to meet his friends. He rode out alone to Tara. Now, the djeli do not tell us the details of what happened at that place. They do not recall the names of the heroes of Tara who came out one by one to fight Diuladjan. But the first day Diuladjan defeated twenty challengers, after which he slept. The second day Diuladjan defeated twenty more, after which he slept. The challenges continued five days, and each day Diuladjan killed twenty of the Bambara heroes. And when he had killed one hundred in all, he called for the chief of Tara to come out and speak with him. He said, "I did not come here to despoil your town of its young men. I have killed enough. I came only because I was compelled by honor. I am satisfied. If you wish to continue, I will be patient and stay. If you wish to end the fighting, say to me three times, 'Diuladjan, you have multiplied your honor. Tara applauds your valor. We want it to end.'" The chief of Tara repeated the words three times, after which Diuladjan mounted his horse and went home to Kiban. The story of his accomplishment reached Kiban before Diuladjan did. All the djeli of the town came out to meet him and sing songs of praise.

Nevertheless, Diuladjan remained bitter against Tuba. He thought, "I killed one hundred men at Tara, but the people of that town were not guilty of anything. They fought me one by one and observed all the rules of honor. It is Tuba that should be punished." And at last he went to the chief and the counselors of Kiban and said, "I want to lead an expedition against Tuba for what they have done to us." The authorities of Kiban agreed, and the fighting men made themselves ready.

That same night the counselors of Kiban came to his house to consult him about the war. They found him with his head down and tears coming from his eyes. They asked, "Diuladjan, what is the matter?" He replied, "I am crying because of the consequences of what we are about to do. We have great heroes and Tuba has great heroes. We will fight and many of our great heroes will no longer be alive. Who will be left to defend the Seven Cities against the Bambara and the Fula? Our widows and orphans cannot do it. This war will bring the Seven Cities to their downfall. That is why I am crying." The counselors went to the chief and told him what they had heard from Diuladjan. They discussed it. At last the chief said, "Diuladjan is right. For the sake of the Seven Cities we must call off the expedition."

So, after all, Kiban did not make war against Tuba. But the news of Diuladjan's victory over the town of Tara reached the ears of King Amadu in Segu City. The king said, "Kiban is still a great power. Its heroes are still champions. Tuba is also a great power, but it is not the equal of Kiban." Amadu sent his chief djeli to the Seven Cities of the Soninke to inform them that Kiban would continue to be his administrator of the region. Tuba was not happy. For a brief time it had been first among the Seven Cities, but now once more it was in the shadow of Kiban. Because of Diuladjan Diabi, Kiban remained the foremost of the Soninke cities in the kingdom of Segu.

TUBA'S LAST EFFORT AGAINST KIBAN

DIULADJAN LIVED ON, HE LIVED HIS TIME. Madine Diabe and Bakore Samassa lived on, they lived their time. Other heroes also were born, lived and died. But all the heroes of Kiban left their names in the hearts of the bards. Kiban and Tuba remained where they were standing. Neither city forgot its feelings for the other. Tuba still had envy for Kiban, and Kiban still had bitter thoughts of Tuba, even after the white men came and assumed power over everything.

Tuba thought, "Now that the white men rule, at last we may take our rightful place over Kiban." The city sent an emissary to the white governor in Kulukoro to request that Kiban be placed under the administrative authority of Tuba. The emissary recounted the history of the Seven Cities. He recalled that Tuba had great families and great heroes. When the white governor had heard everything he said, "You have given us something to think about. Wait here in

169

Kulukoro until we have considered it." He spoke to his counselors. They told him, "Yes, Tuba ought to have authority over Kiban."

When news of what was happening reached the ears of Kiban it was received with anger. People exclaimed, "Aaah! Tuba is at it again. We should have put an end to Tuba long ago." The chief of Kiban was Bakari Silla. He said, "Even though the white men have seized power, this matter does not belong to them. It belongs to us. We are Soninke. I will do something. I will make an expedition to Kulukoro. I will take the governor's head. I will take the head of Tuba's emissary. I will take the heads of the treacherous counselors. I will bring you the heads. But if I do not come back you will know that I am dead."

Bakari made himself ready. He went to his morike, who did mystic work to protect Bakari's body from bullets. Bakari hung his gun on his back. He hung across his chest the scabbard containing his long knife. He mounted his horse. He said to his djeli, "Let us go now to visit the governor in Kulukoro." His djeli rode behind him, the way it had always been when heroes went to war. The djeli played his ngoni and sang songs about Bakari's family and the greatness of Kiban.

When Bakari approached the governor's quarters in Kulukoro, people said, "Here comes Bakari of Kiban, his gun on his back, his long knife on his chest, and his djeli playing the ngoni. There will be trouble." The governor asked, "Why should there be trouble?" His counselors said, "There will be trouble because Tuba wants authority over Kiban. Kiban is the greatest of the cities. It will not accept what Tuba wants." The governor said, "We will discuss it." His counselors answered, "You, governor, wish to discuss it with your mouth. Bakari of Kiban comes to discuss with his gun and his long knife. By the manner in which he comes we know that he is ready to take heads." The governor said, "Do you have advice for me?" They answered, "Yes. Do not give Tuba anything. Leave things the way they are."

Bakari entered. The breezes in the bush had not cooled his burning anger. He said, "I am Bakari from Kiban. I came to ask you, white man, whether it is true that you are going to put Tuba over Kiban." The governor replied, "No. What you have heard is only

170

rumor. We will never put Kiban under any other city. Kiban is forever Kiban, paramount among the Seven Cities."

Bakari's right hand was poised to seize the hilt of his long knife, but it did not move. He could not find words. What the governor had said was not what he had expected. He finally spoke, saying, "I hear you. But I ask again." The governor repeated that Tuba would not have any authority over Kiban, and that Kiban would always be Kiban. Bakari asked once more, for a pledge given three times is stronger than iron. And once more he received the same answer.

The fire burning inside Bakari was left with nothing to consume but himself. His eyes closed, and he fell unconscious to the floor. They put cold water to his face and revived him. He stood up. He said to the governor, "Excuse me. I did not foresee your answer. I expected to kill you, your counselors and the emissary from Tuba and take your heads back to Kiban, or to die in the attempt. The first time you spoke, I could not believe what I heard. But you spoke the pledge three times, and the weight of it was too much for me. Now I have nothing more to do here in Kulukoro. I will return to Kiban."

He went out and mounted his horse. He rode away from Kulukoro, his djeli following. The djeli played his ngoni and sang songs praising the greatness of Kiban. He also sang:

> *Bakari, the sword of Kiban.*
> *He asked the white man to judge.*
> *The white man acknowledged it.*
> *He said, "Kiban will never be less than Kiban."*

SELECTIVE GLOSSARY

ALMAMI. A Muslim teacher of the Koran, equivalent to *imam*. Among the Bambara the *almami* was also called *morike*. Although the Bambara were animists and fetishists, and although they resisted the intrusion of Muslim populations and beliefs as a matter of ideological and political policy, the services of *almamis* or *morikes* were in great demand in Segu. Many of them were of Fula or Soninke origin, and some came from more distant parts of the Sudan. According to the explorer Mungo Park, there were numerous mosques in Segu City in the time of King Da Monzon. See under MORIKE.

AZAN. The muezzin's call to prayer.

BA. A homonym meaning either river or mother. Also signifies "great" or "distinguished," as in *djeliba*, meaning "great *djeli*."

BAMANA. See BAMBARA.

BAMBARA. One of a number of tribes of the Mande group, which includes the Soninke, the Manding (Mandinka), the Bozo and others. The Bambara coexisted with these tribes and others, such as the Fula, from early times, and all were components of the Ghana and Mali empires. The Bambara—in some dialects called Bamana—founded the kingdom of Segu early in the seventeenth century. A little later they founded a second kingdom, called Kaarta, a short distance to the north.

BASSI. A cereal dish made mainly of millet meal or flour. (Also the name of a king of Samaniana.)

BULO. An outer chamber or anteroom of the residence of a king, chief or wealthy person. The narrations say that the royal residence in Segu had six adjoining *bulos* through which one had to pass to reach the courtyard in which the king's personal living quarters were located.

DJELI. Professional bard-historians with hereditary ties to noble families. (Singular and plural are given the same spelling, in accordance with the usage of the narrators.) The word *djeli* also means "blood," signifying this hereditary relationship. The *djeli* sang the chronicles of the noble families, were consulted on questions of geneology, and often were used as family emissaries. A king's *djeli* acted as "linguist" or "transmitter of words" in formal court situations.

DJIBEDJAN. A ceremonial horse used by the king of Segu on important ceremonial occasions. It was never ridden at other times.

DJURU. A generic term referring to various kinds of praise songs. See under WOLOSEKORO.

FILELIKELA. A Bambara practitioner of the mystic sciences. He was a diviner and a maker of defensive and aggressive magic, equivalent to the *morike* except that he did not use Koranic knowledge in his work. See under MORIKE.

FULA. One of the tribes of the Sudan that played a significant part in the ebb and flow of the early Ghana and Mali empires. In some usages, Fulani is the collective term for the Fula, also known as the Peuhl. At the time of the kingdom of Segu, the Fula were predominantly Muslim.

GARAN. A hobble made of rope, used on the forelegs of horses to keep them from straying. In some of the narrations the *garan* is given magical powers by a *morike* so that it may be used as a deadly weapon.

GARANKE. A leatherworker, member of a hereditary class (i.e., caste) of Bambara craftsmen who prepared hides for various uses and made objects of leather and other nonmetallic materials.

GUIBARA. A fermented drink made of honey.

KAWRAW. A homonym meaning either "brother" or "old."

MARAKA. A Sudanic tribe, usually called Marka by Europeans. Some Sudanese consider the Maraka to be an offshoot of the Bambara, others to be a branch of the Soninke. See also under SONINKE.

MORIKE. Also called *mori, karamoki, karamokoke* or, loosely, *almami*. The *morike* was a teacher of the Koran and also a practitioner of the mystic sciences. Because of his Koranic knowledge, the *morike* (often of non-Bambara origin) was believed to be especially powerful in divining and in the making of protective and aggressive magic. See under FILELIKELA and ALMAMI.

NGONI. A plucked stringed instrument commonly used by *djeli* to accompany historical or praise songs.

NUMUKE. A blacksmith and craftsman in gold and silver. Sometimes called simply *numu*. (*Ke* = man.) The *numuke* worked primarily in iron, and was involved in every stage of iron making, beginning with smelting. He made farming tools, weapons and various workaday implements. In addition, he carved masks, fetish figures and other wooden objects. All metalwork was done by the *numu* caste. The *numuke* was also the official who performed circumcisions.

THE PRICE-OF-THE-HONEY. An annual tax, usually paid to the king in cowries, sometimes in gold or silver. The name derives from an earlier tax paid in the form of honey. Tradition says that King Biton Mamari Kulibali put an end to the honey tax and decreed that cowries of equal worth be substituted.

SARAKA. Charity, an act of charity.

SONINKE. One of the major tribes of the Mande group in the Western Sudan. The Soninke people are sometimes called Sarakole, and by some Bambara they are referred to as Maraka. The Soninke were the probable founders of the ancient empire of Ghana. By the time that the kingdom of Segu appeared, the Soninke had accepted Muslim belief, although they retained significant elements of their pre-Islamic cultural traditions.

TAFO. A talisman or amulet.

WOLOSEKORO. A Bambara style of musical composition sung and played on the *ngoni* by the *djeli* to honor a brave person. It is one of several types of *djuru* (meaning "cord") performed by *djeli*. Another form of *djuru*, called *djoba*, was played and sung only for the king. According to tradition, a king's *djoba* was played for him only twice, once at the time of his enthronement and once after his death.

SELECTED BACKGROUND READINGS

Baohen, A. Adu. "Kingdoms of West Africa," in *The Horizon History of Africa*. New York: American Heritage Publishing Co., 1971.

Bérenger-Féraud, L. *Les Peuplades de la Sénégambie*. Paris, 1879.

Courlander, Harold. "Three Soninke Tales," in *African Arts*, XII, 1, November 1978.

———. *Tales of Yoruba Gods and Heroes: Myths, Legends and Heroic Tales of the Yoruba People of West Africa*. New York: Crown Publishers, 1973.

Davidson, Basil. *History of West Africa to the Nineteenth Century*. New York: Doubleday and Co., Anchor Books edition, 1966.

———. "The Niger to the Nile," in *The Horizon History of Africa*. New York: American Heritage Publishing Co., 1971.

Du Bois, W. E. Burghardt. *Black Folk Then and Now*. New York: Henry Holt and Co., 1939.

Frobenius, Leo, and Douglas C. Fox. *African Genesis*. New York: Stackpole Sons, 1937.

Haywood, A. *Through Timbuctu and Across the Great Sahara*. London, 1912.

Henry, Joseph. *L'ame d'un Peuple Africain, les Bambara*. Münster: Bibliothèque Anthropos, 1910.

Ibn-Battuta. "Voyage dans le Soudan," translated by M. Slane, in *Journal Asiatique*, 1843.

———. *Voyages*. Translated by C. Defrémery and B. R. Sarguinetti. Paris, 1922.

Imperato, Pascal J. "Bamana and Maninka Twin Figures," in *African Arts*, VIII, 4, Summer 1975.

———. "Bambara and Malinke Ton Masquerades," in *African Arts*, XIII, 4, August 1980.

Jobson, R. *The Golden Trade: or, a Discovery of the River Gambra, and the Golden Trade of the Aethiopians*. London, 1823.

Laude, Jean. *The Arts of Black Africa*, translated by Jean Decock. Berkeley: University of California Press, 1971.

McNaughton, Patrick R. "Bamana Blacksmiths," in *African Arts*, XII, 2, February 1979.

Middleton, John. *Peoples of Africa*. New York: Arco Publishing Co., 1978.

Monteil, Charles. *Les Bambara de Ségou et du Kaarta*. Paris: Larose, 1924.

Park, Mungo. *Travels in Africa*. London: J. M. Dent and Sons, 1954, 1969. (Early editions, published in London, appeared in 1799 and 1815.)

Tauxier, Louis. *Histoire des Bambaras*. Paris, 1942.

Wiener, Leo. *Africa and the Discovery of America*, Vol. III. Philadelphia: Innes and Sons, 1922.